P9-APT-729

THE ART OF THEATRE-GOING

THE ART OF THEATRE-GOING

BY

JOHN DRINKWATER

BOSTON AND NEW YORK
HOUGHTON MIFFLIN COMPANY
The Riverside Press Cambridge
1927

The Riverside Press

CAMBRIDGE · MASSACHUSETTS

PRINTED IN THE U.S.A.

TO
ALFRED SUTRO

PREFACE FOR AMERICAN EDITION

THE purpose of this book is chiefly to define some general principles of the theatre by means of examples drawn from my own experience as an actor, producer, dramatist, and playgoer. In order to make these examples as precise as possible I have, as an Englishman, necessarily had to confine my attention for the most part to the English theatre as I have known it in my own lifetime. But the principles themselves, if sound, should be applicable to any other playgoer's experience, and particularly in America, where the average year's showing of the theatre is very much like our own. The fact that I have drawn hardly at all upon the American theatre for my purposes will, I hope, not make any argument less pertinent to my American friends. After all, it would be a poor thing for the prospects of this book if even my English readers were confined to playgoers whose experience of the play had coincided exactly with my own. It is no less true of criticism than of art that a general argument gains by being drawn from a particular instance whether the instance happens to be widely known before the argument or not.

Since 1921 I have been fortunate enough to see a good deal of the American theatre, and it could readily have furnished me with some of my illustrations. But, in spite of the fact that there is nowadays so much in common between the English stage and the American, there are differences of method and convention, and it was wiser for me to speak of the environment with which I have been familiar by long contact. The remarks which, as an Englishman, I make in the following pages concerning the Irish Players are applicable in some degree to the American stage as seen through English eyes. When I go into an American theatre, although the play may be one of a kind to which I am quite used, there is always a certain air of novelty that to some extent clouds the judgment. One of the most striking experiences that I have ever had in a theatre was the performance of *Outside Looking In* given in New York some two or three years ago. That this was in many respects a very remarkable production I am convinced. But it seemed to make but a limited appeal to Americans, and it may be that to my English eyes and ears it displayed qualities of freshness that were not so apparent to playgoers more familiar with its idiom of speech and character. This raises one of the æsthetic problems of the theatre that I have here discussed at some length.

In more general terms, the artistic and economic conditions of the American theatre are, so far as

I know them, much the same as those prevailing in England. The greater wealth of America ensures on the whole, I think, a greater efficiency of production than is commonly attained in England. Executive ability is inevitably attracted by money, and there is neither sense nor reason in complaining of this. The motive is not merely a mercenary one; executive ability wants the best mechanical assistance that it can find, and money provides this. But while I think that the general level of production in New York is higher than that of London I do not think that there is anything to choose between the best in either case. The American theatre of entertainment, governed by commercial considerations, will with its greater resources bring off more successes than its London competitor. And I suppose that with its more drastic methods it will also record a large number of disasters. But the fortunes of this theatre are not in any case of serious interest to anyone but the promoters. In the theatre of the imagination, on the other hand, we find a remarkable, though instinctive, co-ordination of aim. Each year sees, both in New York and London, the production of two or three plays that help to keep the drama among the significant arts, and in most of them there is nothing but a turn — often a considerable turn — of an inflection to show whether the work is American or English. The

Repertory or Little Theatres, again, have had the same problems to face in both countries, have suffered from the same limitations, and have achieved much the same success. In nothing, perhaps, is a common spirit in artistic endeavour shown more clearly to-day than in the spread and influence of community drama throughout the United States and England.

Informed opinion is making more and more for Anglo-American friendship and even affection. But this association depends not on a sentimental confusion of interests but upon a clear recognition of contrasts. We are happily learning to accept these contrasts for what they are worth, not unhumorously, and at the same time to respect them. But, with no sympathy for such confusions, we may still allow that races with, approximately, a common language, must find a great bond in their literature. It is no matter for surprise that in drama, which shares with fiction the privilege of being literature's most democratic form, we see a constant and amicable exchange, not only between Broadway and the West End but between the wider ranges of the United States and Great Britain. John Millington Synge and John Galsworthy and Eugene O'Neill do not meet as strangers. But this is to embark upon a topic beyond the purpose of the present study, and my Preface is meant to be no more than an invitation to American playgoers to spend a few hours with me in the English theatre, where I think they may come to conclusions not much unlike those formed in their own.

JOHN DRINKWATER

LONDON, *May*, 1927

CONTENTS

THE ART OF THEATRE-GOING

THE ART OF THEATRE-GOING

APPROACH TO THE THEATRE

THIS book is intended to be neither a history of drama nor of the theatre, though historical references will necessarily come within its design. My own experiences as a playgoer have no doubt been partly conditioned by the fact that for some years I was a daily worker in the theatre, as actor, producer, manager, and even on occasion as designer, and by my continued occupation as a playwright; but it is as a playgoer that I now wish to approach my subject. And since playgoing, while it may be said to be the most popular of intellectual diversions, is also in many respects perhaps the most personal, I shall be forgiven if I indulge somewhat freely in allusions to those performances that I happen to have seen myself.

I say most personal, because once a performance is over and we have not seen it, we cannot ever have a trustworthy idea of what it was like, even by the aid of the most competent report. If a book is recommended to me, I can test it for myself at any time. And if I am told that a play is a good one, I can see it when it is next produced, or perhaps read it. But if I tell you that the most moving performance of Shakespeare that I ever saw was that of 'Measure for Measure' given by Miss Horniman's company under Mr. William Poel's direction at Stratford-upon-Avon in 1908, what meaning has the assertion for you unless you were there too, which almost certainly you were not?

Thus, at the outset, we are confronted by the chief difficulty that besets all talk about the theatre. How often does the young critic — or the old one — tell us with an air of finality that Miss A. or Mr. B. gave positively the finest performance that it has ever been his good fortune to witness, implying thereby that here is unquestionably the most remarkable histrionic talent that has hitherto revealed itself? But what does the young, or the old, critic know about it? Mr. John Barrymore is his fancy — very well, a likely choice. But did he ever see Henry Irving? He did. Then what about Phelps, or Kean? Yes, even them. But Garrick? And before Garrick, was there not Burbage? And who among us, in these conditions, can have any standards ampler than those formed by personal preferences and an experience that at best is drastically limited? We can, for example, base our judgment on any poem that we read on a natural taste reinforced by a working acquaintance with the representative achievement of poetry as a whole; we may even do the same thing in respect of drama as a written word. But of drama acted, that is to say of drama in its proper expression, we can judge only by casual and fragmentary knowledge. Even the professional playgoer, who spends four nights a week in the theatre season in and season out, can only judge performances by the standards of his own immediate moment, standards that are in fact hardly standards at all, since they are referable to no real comparative tests. A veteran, such as Mr. Walkley, could decide for himself whether Mr. Nicholas Hannen was or was not as good an actor as Sir Charles Wyndham, but his opinion could mean nothing to young playgoers who never saw Wyndham, and Mr. Walkley himself could not tell how either of them compared with James Wallack. There are many young playgoers for whom in fifty years' time Miss Gladys Cooper and Miss Sybil Thorndike will be remembered as glories of the golden age of the theatre, and for whom the splendid triumphs of Dame Ellen Terry will mean nothing.

CRITICISM AND ACTING

EACH generation, each decade, one might almost say each season, has, therefore, to be a sufficient criterion to itself in this matter of stage performances. Even the travel bore who dilates on places you have never visited is less tedious than the theatre bore who comes at you with players you have never seen. This is why nearly all criticism of acting is unreadable, or meaningless if read. The only criticism of acting that is not a waste of paper and printers' ink is that which combines an ability to write with a technical knowledge of acting, and while every dramatic critic now in practice may be a master in the former respect, I do not know of more than three who are not children in the latter. This is not to say that the critics, most of them, do not know a good or bad performance when they see it, but that they are unable to tell us — or the actors — anything worth while about it. In this the critic is in precisely the same position as the ordinary playgoer, the difference being that one gets paid for going and the other pays to go to the theatre. It is exceptional to find either of them distinguishing between the part and the player, seeing how much or how little the player has brought to the author's intention, realising how easy one part is and how difficult another, or remembering that it is absurd to say of any normally competent production that the best acting of the evening came from someone who was on the stage for ten minutes. Both are, in fact, controlled almost entirely by impressions in the theatre. As both are members of the audience, it is entirely proper that in the theatre they should be so controlled — that is the function of the audience, and is marked by applause or cat-calls. But when one of them leaves the theatre and turns critic, his function undergoes an important change. For the ordinary playgoer the impressions received in the theatre are enough, and when he tells us of them we ask no more than the most unsophisticated translation into words. 'Jolly good,' or 'rotten,' is all we need or should expect from him. But the critic parts company with his neighbour in the stalls and takes on the rôle of expert. His duty now is to translate his impressions not into terms of corresponding simplicity, but into an exact and reasoned argument. 'Jolly good' and 'rotten' will not serve his purpose at all. If my barber uses these appraisements, I am interested; but if an expert, whose opinion I buy, uses them, I think that I am being fobbed off with an impertinence. It is his business to tell me why he thinks a performance was jolly good or rotten, which is what he hardly ever does.

And in most cases the reason is that he does not know.

It is this question of acting, more than that of the drama itself, that perplexes playgoing. We in the audience know so much, and yet we know so little. In the first place, our impressions may, generally speaking, be relied on to be sound. We have no means of saying whether the players before us are as good as those who performed for Ben Jonson or Congreve, but we are not in the least likely to decide that Mr. Ivor Novello is a better actor than Mr. Fred Terry.[1] A good performance of a play is certain, with a negligible margin of error, to excite an audience to approval, and a bad one to leave it manifestly cold. Even the differences of opinion, often violent, existing within the audience itself, will not materially affect the conclusion. But when the ordinary playgoer talks about his impressions afterwards, he often finds himself ashamed of the limitations of jolly good or rotten, and seeks to justify himself as an intelligent being with some more explicit analysis. And then the trouble begins. Irrelevant trifles obtrude themselves upon his recollection. In the theatre he has been enthralled, but now he remembers that Malvolio spoke more quickly than usual — too quickly that is — that Orsino had thin legs, that in consecutive scenes the sun rose

[1] Which still leaves room for him to be a very good one.

and set in the same place, that Viola really was ridiculously unlike Sebastian, that Curio forgot his lines and that the holy father had actually forgotten to take his wrist watch off, that Toby Belch had too much blood on his pate and Feste's voice wasn't half as good as Caruso's or Mr. McCormack's. None of these things troubled him for a moment at the time; he has, indeed, just told you that the performance was jolly good. But pressed by enquiry, or his own self-respect, to enlarge on that, these are the things that seem to be all that can loosen his tongue; and in ten minutes he is well on the way to believing that it was not so jolly good after all. To explain why it was good is a very subtle process, demanding not only receptivity but insight, not only a sound heart but technical knowledge. In default of these qualifications, he abandons the unequal task, and betakes himself to the much easier one of telling us concisely what were the defects. And these defects, of no importance whatever, occupy his mind, until they dominate it. In translating his emotion into terms of reason he has hopelessly falsified the original impression that he received with all the admirable power of his nature. He has been a good playgoer and a futile critic. He is not to be blamed, and he does little if any harm; provided always that he does not make a public demonstration of his futility and ask to be indemnified for his pains.

The consequence of this uncertainty among public and critics alike is that while good acting is sure of popular favour the only possible way in which we can enjoy it is to see it. The instructed and instructive account of it is so rare as virtually not to exist. Not that it is unachievable. I have heard a dramatist, who not only appreciates acting but understands it, describe — not imitate — a performance by an old player in such a way as to communicate something of the original delight. When Lamb writes of Bensley, 'He seized the moment of passion with the greatest truth; like a faithful clock, never anticipating or leading you to anticipate. He was totally destitute of trick or artifice. He seemed come upon the stage to do the poet's message simply. . . . He let the passion or the sentiment do its own work without prop or bolstering. He would have scorned to mountebank it; and betrayed none of that *cleverness* which is the bane of serious acting' — when Charles Lamb writes this we know the kind of actor that Bensley was; and when he writes further, that he 'threw over the part an air of Spanish loftiness. . . . It was big and swelling, but you could not be sure that it was hollow. You might wish to see it taken down, but you felt that it was upon an elevation,' we begin to have a very good idea of how Bensley played Malvolio, an idea that develops as Lamb proceeds. Or again, is not

Munden more than a name, a comedian in being, as we learn from the same critic that 'when you think he has exhausted his battery of looks . . . suddenly he sprouts out an entirely new set of features, like Hydra. He is not one, but legion. . . . He, and he alone, literally *makes faces*. . . . [His] gusto antiquates and ennobles what it touches. His pots and his ladles are as grand and primal as the seething-pots and hooks seen in old prophetic vision. A tub of butter, contemplated by him, amounts to a Platonic idea. . . . He stands wondering, amid the common-place materials of life, like primæval man with the sun and stars about him.'

And to take one more example, from our own time, consider this from Mr. Shaw. 'Luckily "Les Surprises de Divorce" had been made famous by Coquelin, the greatest comedian known to us. Mr. Hare had by no means the worst of the comparison in point of execution. . . . Coquelin clowned [a particular scene], even to the length of bounding into the air and throwing forward his arms and legs as if to frighten off some dangerous animal. But he did not produce the electric effect of Mr. Hare's white, tense face and appalled stare, conveying somehow a mad speed of emotion and a frightful suspense of action never to be forgotten by any playgoer with the true dramatic memory. Coquelin's compensation in the comparison lay in the greater fullness of his contribution to the drama. He played between the lines, and quadrupled the value of the part: Mr. Hare, with his swift, crisp method, and his habit of picking up a cue as if it were a cricket-ball to be smartly fielded, only made the most of the play as it was.'

Even to me, who know nothing about the play in question, who never saw Coquelin and Sir John Hare only once in my childhood, Mr. Shaw conveys a definite idea of the contrasted methods that those actors brought to a given part. It is true that he is reduced to the expedient of declaring that Hare could never be forgotten in the part by anyone who had seen him, which is not of much assistance to anyone who hasn't, but there is nevertheless in Mr. Shaw's criticism a sense of acting, and it is somehow conveyed to us. The passage does not display the nicety and visualising power that we find in those taken from Lamb, but if the average of dramatic criticism in regard to acting could touch its quality the standard would be immeasurably higher than it is. And this is not merely to say that it would be a good thing if all our critics were as great as Mr. Shaw, because I do not think that in the famous collection of 'Dramatic Opinions' Mr. Shaw is a great critic. As a dramatist I think that he is in many important respects, and in spite of abrupt limitations, the most considerable force that has enlivened our theatre for two hundred years, but as a critic he was, as he himself may be said to confess, a brilliant crusader whose way was to proclaim a gospel of his own by deriding and bedevilling any other truth that happened to get in his way. This made for splendid entertainment, and has kept 'Dramatic Opinions' fresh and sparkling while most — if not all — of the other dramatic journalism of its day has gone safely to the worms.

But great criticism is not made that way. Mr. Shaw at any moment might say something that the greatest critic might have coveted, but he was never safe not to say something that had not even a superficial air of being reasonable. And if you can't rely on your man's opinions, he is not, for you, the great critic. It is not a case of agreeing with them but of being confident that, agree or not, you will find them responsibly founded, even though you sometimes think they are mistaken. Mr. Shaw's opinions could be exquisitely instructive, but they could also be plainly irresponsible, so that in reading his essays we are sure of immense fun, sure of frequent illumination, but never sure that he won't let us down. In conceiving him as a standard for dramatic criticism, therefore, we are not asking for the moon. His work as a critic had too many faults to secure it in too exalted a place, and human infirmity need not despair before such an example. But Mr. Shaw knew — happily still knows — what acting was, and realised that if he was going to set up as a writer on the subject — we must remember that he did this explicitly in preparation for his work as a playwright — he must be able to convey his impressions to his readers in reasoned terms. He did not suppose that he could do his job properly by saying 'Mr. —— in the part of —— gave the best performance that we have had from a young actor on the London stage for the last five years.'

THE CRITICS

If anyone should suppose that this is intended as an attack on the critics, let me assure him that it isn't. I think the critics are much to be pitied. They may enjoy themselves greatly in the theatre, in spite of repeated discouragement, but clearly they have the devil of a time outside it. The public demands, or at least editors believe that the public demands it, that the notice of a play shall contain extended reference to the acting. The critic, therefore, has to supply this, and a maddening job it must be. In the first place, of at least one half of the acting that he sees there is nothing intelligent to be said, chiefly because no occasion for the exercise of intelligent acting has been given by the play. Secondly, if there is something of the kind to be said, nothing, as we have seen, is much more difficult than to say it, apart from the accidental difficulty of having in most cases to say it after about a quarter of an hour's reflection in a taxicab. Thirdly, when, and if, he has said it, there can be at best precious little satisfaction in writing about something that most people can't see to-day and everybody will have forgotten to-morrow.

Even the swells like Lamb, when they are writing about acting, may make us exclaim upon their skill, and yet leave us unmoved. I admire greatly the deftness of mind with which Lamb presents Bensley to us; also I am always deeply stirred by great or even good acting; but Lamb himself does not really make me care twopence what Bensley was like. I take Lamb's word for it, charmed that it is so ingenious a word, and contentedly leave it at that. But when Lamb writes not about the old actors but the old dramatists, my attention is engaged to quite another tune. Then I can not only admire, but approve, contest, amplify my own experience, and learn afresh. No; to write about acting, and to do it as a daily habit, must be as dispiriting an occupation as can fall to a man of wit.

My purpose in introducing the critics at all in this preamble is that their experience serves to show how bewildering for our inexperience this problem of acting is. After all, critics are not stupider than other people because they are compelled to make public exhibitions of their stupidity. The average playgoer who thinks the critic a foolish fellow may reflect with advantage that he would almost certainly be much foolisher in the critic's place. The critic commonly fails in a desperate undertaking, but he is in most cases far better equipped for making a success of it than the playgoing loungers who set themselves up as his critics in turn. He is, indeed, usually not well enough equipped to make a success of it. He doesn't know enough, he hasn't seen enough, and he doesn't get time to think enough. But he does, generally, know more about the drama, he has seen more performances, and he does think more about these things than his average reader. And if he is so hard put to it to make reasonable head and tail of his impressions, how badly will the average reader, with his relatively limited experience, fare for himself? Very badly indeed, we may surmise. And so it is.

Heartily emotional playgoing is common enough; it leads out its tens of thousands nightly. But intelligent playgoing is extremely rare. Up to a point there is no harm in this. It is the commoner mood by which the theatre always has and always must live. In a sense, too, its judgment is good. It frequently patronises to a depressing extent a kind of entertainment that some of us may think a demonstrably inferior kind, but it rarely confuses the good of a kind with the bad. I would, for example, with all my passion for the theatre, rather play billiards or arrange postage stamps or go to bed any time than watch 'Rose Marie'; but I am not so simple as to suppose that 'Rose Marie' has filled a huge theatre for two years for any other reason than that it is a highly efficient show of its own sort. The heartily emotional playgoing population is very generous, but it can't be bluffed into accepting incompetence, and for that it deserves respect. Its tastes are infinitely varied, embracing every range of theatrical fare from Euripides to Mr. Charlot. The audience that sits spellbound at a representation of 'The Trojan Women' is not, that is to say, necessarily a whit more intelligent than the audience that ogles deliriously back at the Ziegfeld Follies. Both are alike primarily dominated by the heartily emotional mood, and the former is likely, in view of its past experiences, to be rather less exacting than the latter in the matter of executive standards. Mr. Ziegfolly is so certain to be up to scratch, while 'The Trojan Women' notoriously isn't.

But if this were all, we should have to accept the position that you just go to the sort of theatre that pleases you, and that it isn't any use arguing about it. And yet, unless we argue about it, some of us find that we are consistently bilked of what we consider to be our dues in the theatre, and it is this that makes intelligent playgoing as distinguished from the other kind a thing to be encouraged; and, first of all, to be encouraged in ourselves. If I go to a show of the Ziegfeld Follies, I like it; if I go to Mr. Granville-Barker's production of 'The Winter's Tale,' I like it. But if I don't get beyond that in my mind about the two occasions, I shall soon be up Queer Street, and, what is more, Mr. Granville-Barker and his productions — using them as an illustration — will be up Queer Street with me. For — and this brings us to a salient in our argument — the one entertainment belongs to the world of easy and pleasurable relaxation, and the other to the world of the imagination. In the one, the theatre is exercising a rightful office in distracting the attention of a wearied public mind, doing it admirably, and in a way that we can all enjoy. But in the other, the theatre is asserting its right to a place among the great constructive arts. All that Mr. Ziegfeld needs is expertness in his own enterprise — a very intricate expertness — to ensure a wide and continued popular support. The people must have this kind of diversion in some form or another, and the man who can provide it is as sure of custom as the efficient food salesman or clothier. But the kingdom of the imagination has to be fought for — not only enjoyed by the emotions, but defended and advanced by the intelligence.

And how difficult this exercise of the intelligence is in the theatre, is seen by the mental contortions to which trained and experienced critics are reduced when confronted by that presiding problem of the theatre — acting; for, unless we get right about this, we cannot hope to recover ourselves by enlightened consideration of the play. The whole art of the theatre is degraded when the actor is considered as an individuality apart from the play in which he is acting. The art of the theatre includes the drama; it does not consist wholly of it, but it includes it, and it can never achieve greatly unless this is recognised as a fundamental condition. When it is forgotten, as it so often is, one of two things will happen. Either you will have the one-man show, such as flourishes in the music-halls, or you will have a fustian theatre furnished by hack playwrights at the bidding of powerful and popular stars. In the first place there is no reason for complaint. The mastery of such men as Wilkie Bard and George Formby and Bert Williams needs no apology. To miss its appeal is as dull as to confuse it with greater things. But in the theatre that professes an allegiance to the art of the dramatist, it is another matter. Even there, when the play is frankly and shamelessly made the occasion of what is in effect nothing but a succession of one-man or one-woman turns, it makes, as they say, no matter. The revues and musical comedies are variants of the music-halls, and well enough as such. But the trouble is that the theatre in which some allegiance to the imagination is still professed is corrupted when this dissociation of the actor from his environment is allowed. Here I must explain what I mean when I speak of the theatre of the imagination. I do not claim that my definition is a satisfactory one for everybody; I merely wish to be clear as to what I intend to convey when I use a term that will occur frequently in this essay.

All arts are in constant danger of becoming commercialised, and none more so than that of the theatre. This is truer than ever to-day, when vast capital interests are involved in an enterprise that means no more to the financiers than any other form of speculation. It is now possible for one man to own six reputable London theatres, some of them with distinguished traditions, and make no pretensions to any taste or even interest in the drama. Clearly his policy will be either to let his theatres at a guaranteed rental, or to pay subordinates to fill them with such forms of entertainment as are in the current fashion. Out of six such productions he can rely on handsome profits from, say, four, and he can comfortably afford to cut his losses on the other two. In either case he is a parasitic and crippling growth upon the theatre, destroying enterprise and discouraging the individual manager. This, definitely, is commercialism of an art, and its prevalence to-day is common knowledge. But at the foundations of every art, no matter how commercialised it may become, is the imagination of which I speak. An artist has some genuinely personal vision of life, and he finds himself moulding it into intelligible form, without reference to possible profit or reputation for himself. That, as I see it, is an act of the imagination. That he actively concerns himself afterwards with the commercial welfare of his work does not effect the question; at the time of creation the service of the imagination is his only purpose. Such artists have at intervals gone into the theatre, and of these occasions has been produced the great body of drama that enriches the literature of the world. It is in them that the art of the theatre[1] has its

[1] For purposes of this book, I mean the theatre as we English-speaking people have known it for five hundred years or so.

origins, the art that no commercialisation can ever wholly destroy.

The one-man show is, frankly, an exploitation of personality; often a very engaging personality. But the theatre of the imagination must be more than this. When we find a theatre that makes a formal acknowledgment of the drama and yet is in fact devoted to this same kind of exploitation, we know that something calamitous is happening. Henry Irving was for many years the head of the theatrical profession in England. When I was sixteen I ran from my office at closing time and stood for two hours or more in a queue outside a Birmingham theatre holding ninepence with which to pay for early door admission to the gallery. This was to see Irving. When I reached the box-office window the 'gallery full' board was put out. In despair I begged to be allowed to try my luck, and at last succeeded in getting my metal token — cut, I remember, like a rosicrucian cross — for ninepence. When I had climbed the stairs, I found every inch of standing room occupied to the back wall, and could see nothing but the dimly lit timbers of a lofty dome. After furtive and vain efforts to squeeze myself into some corner of vantage, I somehow climbed up the back wall, swarmed along a beam on my stomach, and lay the entire evening on a six-inch accumulation of dust, peering down from the roof on to a stage that seemed to be a mile away. And I would, if I could, do the same thing again to-night in order to see Henry Irving act. For there *was* acting if you like, as I may tell any young playgoer who never saw it. But underneath the glamour of that histrionic genius, what did we find after all but the one-man show *in excelsis?* Instead, however, of being frankly that, this, we were asked to believe, was the theatre that took its place among the great arts. As a one-man show it was magnificent, but as the theatre of the imagination, we sadly realised that, for all its pomp and ceremony, it did not exist. For acting, be it as rich as you will in native ability and power, does not become great until it is employed in the service of great drama. A man like Irving could so invest the dregs of impoverished play-writing with his own superb quality as to make us forget the wretched stuff in which he was dealing, but on reflection we realised that Irving's genius labouring against enormous odds was by no means compensation for what we ought to have had, namely, such a genius devoted to the service of yet greater and more significant genius than itself. In other words, Irving's personality and conception of life as expressed with consummate skill in his acting, were well worth anybody's attention, but it is no use pretending that they were of anything like the organic importance of a play by Shakespeare. And even when Irving played Shakespeare, the exploitation persisted. The play was adapted, brilliantly adapted, to the purposes of that same personality. It was not the interpretation of a great drama that was offered, but the compulsory submission of a great dramatist to the needs of a man who had all the equipment of a great actor and seldom cared to use it. Leaving Shakespeare out of the reckoning, what play was added in Irving's theatre to the durable stock of English drama? It is useless to say that there were no fine dramatists. Irving could have made fine dramatists if he had wanted them. Half the best poets and novelists of his time would have jumped at an invitation from him, and under his encouragement some of them would have mastered the theatre to their purposes. But Irving was not concerned in their purposes, he was concerned in his own. So was George Formby, but there was no pretence that he was anything else, while Irving stood in the public mind, with his own consent, for the best theatre that we had, the theatre of the imagination. And the bill was not footed.

I will give another example of my meaning, and I hope I may do so without the smallest offence to a very charming and promising young actress. There was recently a production of 'Romeo and Juliet' in London, with Miss Jean Forbes-Robertson in the part of Juliet. It was generally allowed that the production was a poor one, largely, it may be conceded, because of limited time and opportunity. But the occasion was commonly hailed by the critics as a triumph because it had given Miss Forbes-Robertson an opportunity of trying her paces in one of the classic parts. If a professional audition had been in question, this attitude would have been all very well. But it was not a professional audition, it was a public performance of one of the supreme master-pieces of young poetic drama, and as such it seemed to me to be no more than a preposterous travesty. Every time a great play is performed, that play is newly on its trial, and it is a deep disloyalty to the dramatist to use his work in public as a testing ground for ambitious talent. Miss Forbes-Robertson's talent is indubitable, and as Juliet she did many right and sensitive things. There were, too, other meritable moments in the production, provided chiefly, perhaps, by Mr. Loraine as Mercutio. But all this cannot excuse the fact that a beautiful work of the imagination was maimed and stripped and cast by the wayside. Miss Forbes-Robertson would, I am sure, be the first to acknowledge that her talent, on which such high hopes are so reasonably set, is of less consequence than 'Romeo and Juliet.' It is, indeed, only in the service of such creative completeness that her talent can hope to reach its full and happy realisation. In the performance of which I speak nothing approaching creative completeness was ever arrived at, and the talent was left struggling without moorings and without direction. For direction cannot be given to the performance of a great part by individual ability. It can be achieved only by the aid of a compact and well-proportioned interpretation of the play as a whole. When we have that, then, and then only, does great or even fine acting come into its opportunities. This performance of 'Romeo and Juliet' was a medley of one-man shows, of some interest in themselves, but wholly failing to give any adequate idea of the play represented. In face of this transgression, the display of individual talent seemed to some of us to be of little consequence. The pity of it is that many of the experts were ready to dismiss the major failure with a perfunctory word and proclaim that an individual performance of promise or achievement had made the evening a memorable one. For myself it was not a memorable one at all, but an exceedingly unpleasant one, and this in spite of the fact that I was convinced that Miss Forbes-Robertson justified at least half the complimentary things that were said of her, which means that she ought to have a very handsome career ahead.

This is what I mean when I say that the whole art of the theatre is degraded when the actor is considered as an individuality apart from the play in which he is acting. The just fusion of the actor with his part in our minds does not necessitate the common mistake of not realising what the part is doing with the actor or the actor with the part. There are many parts, especially small parts, so effectively placed in the context of the play that it is almost impossible for a competent actor to fail in them. In such a case, to see a remarkable performance where there is in fact an actor-proof part, is an extravagance of criticism. By actor-proof I mean proof for any actor who is worthy of the name; such parts, for example, as Buckingham, Jaques, Dogberry, Caius, Annie Roberts in 'Strife,' Lane in 'The Importance of Being Earnest,' or Burgess in 'Candida.' On the other hand, there are many exceedingly fine parts, mostly long ones, that tax the technical resources of the most experienced and accomplished actor; such parts as Rosalind, Orlando, Edward Voysey, Morell, Rebecca West or Rose Trelawny. Many players have made partial failures in parts such as these while putting ten times as much understanding and invention into their performances as the small part men who have walked off with all the critical bouquets. To say that Mr. A played minimus perfectly and that Mr. B played maximus far from perfectly may be just criticism, but in nine cases out of ten we shall be off the mark if we infer that Mr. A showed himself to be a better actor than Mr. B.

To fuse the actor and the part in our minds is, then, one thing, and to confuse them quite another. The confusion leads commonly to personal injustice, and the fusion is a first necessity in a hopeful approach to the theatre of the imagination. The ever-spreading popular interest in the personality of favourite actors is a phenomenon that we cannot help, however much we may deplore it. The one hopeful sign is that we sometimes find that after all the favourite actor loses his favour if his plays are too shamelessly bad. There is, I suppose, hardly an actor in London to-day who can be sure of drawing a considerable public on the strength of his personality alone, unless he belongs specifically to the one-man show order and doesn't bother about plays at all. Be this as it may, what is called news-interest in actors is still very great, and actors being human it is not surprising that they should be willing and even eager to exploit it. So that great numbers of playgoers drift into the habit of going to the theatre to see an actor rather than what he is acting, and until that habit is cured the theatre of the imagination remains largely beyond their perceptions. It is here that intelligent playgoing makes its first vital onset. As soon as the playgoer advances from the heartily emotional mood to the intelligent mood, informing the one by the other, he looks not for a favourite actor displaying himself to advantage, but for the interpretation of a significant part in which the personality of the actor beyond that part is forgotten. Then, and then only, can we hope for worthy performances of worthy plays. Let the demand arise and the supply follows, but it is a demand that can be made by the intelligence only. The music-hall turns are entertaining enough when we want that sort of entertainment, just as is a horse race or a prize fight or a football match. But in the theatre — the old word, legitimate, was rather a good one — we want something else, and I would not walk across the road to see the ablest actor in the world wasting his talents on a worthless play. And when I do see a worthless play I am not in the least consoled by the reflection that a star is showing off all his tricks to perfection. I know that a great art is being cheated.

I remember how when I was twenty or so a group of us, under the leadership of Barry Jackson, began to make an eager exploration of the theatre. We cared for the arts, painting, poetry, music, all of them, and we knew from our reading that there was also a great art of the drama, of which the theatre was the reputed home. The glamour of playgoing was on us from the first, and every visit to the theatre was a romance. For me it still is, however damnable may be the operations that go on before me. But always — or nearly always —

with our pleasure there was a sense of dissatisfaction, of frustration. It was so jolly, and yet somehow it did not give us the same delight as we found in the great books, the great pictures, the great symphonies. Was this the art of the theatre? If so, we had to confess that it was a very inferior art to these others that liberated all our adolescent energies. And we did not believe it. We became more and more convinced that the theatre as we saw it was not the right sort of theatre, and that it was betraying a trust. The effect on our minds was curious. For a time we fell to telling each other that the actors whom we saw were bad actors. This, in view of the fact that the provincial favourites of that time included half a dozen of the most expert actors in the country, was illogical, but we were in no mood for logic. All we knew was that the effect made upon us, enchanting as it was, was short in some capital way of what we wanted, and we testily put it down to their acting, through which our impressions were received. We soon learnt better than that, but only to realise that the real trouble was not with the acting but the things acted. The discovery came chiefly, I think, through those magical Shakespeare seasons with the Benson Company at Stratford-upon-Avon. What we should think of them if we saw them now there is no telling, but in those days they were apocalyptic. Here we saw acting beautifully subdued by a band of eager spirits to a common purpose, the reverent and coördinated presentation of a great dramatist's work. Here at last was the true excitement. Each actor had his own following, and very comfortable and friendly it all was, but not one of them ever for a moment forgot that this was Shakespeare's Festival. Shakespeare took hold of that company, possessed them, and transfigured them. There were many shortcomings in the productions. The method paid insufficient heed to Shakespeare's technique, the texts were not too scrupulously handled, and the stage design was of a somewhat chancy character. Cooperation between the theatre and scholarship has done much in the past twenty years to raise the standard in these matters, and Mr. Nugent Monck, Mr. Granville-Barker, Mr. Nigel Playfair and Sir Barry Jackson have all done things that were beyond the resources of Stratford in those days. I do not mention Mr. William Poel in this connection, because he has known the truth about these things as long as I can remember. But for the very spirit of acting directed to the service of our theatre of the imagination those Benson seasons have been excelled by none of them. When Mr. Poel produced 'Hamlet,' he is said to have assembled his company on the stage for prayer before the performance began. The Benson people would have quickened to that, being athletes of the mind and body. But how it would have split the sides of Mr. ——, no, I name no names.

The consequences of our discovery of Stratford in some theatrical enterprises of our own are another story, but I have never forgotten the lessons that I there learnt, and I think my friends would say the same. Having spent part of my infancy travelling round the country with a stock company, and having almost lived in a theatre for several years of my life, the spell binds me for ever. I love all the trappings of the stage, the grease paints, the queer old photographs, such as those that engarland the rooms of Mr. Willy Clarkson's establishment, the rehearsals, the sound of the call-boy, the humours and vexations, the electrician on his perch and the prompter in his corner, and every time I go to the theatre among the audience I get the sense of all these things, so that no evening spent there is quite wasted time for me. But as a playgoer I have never lost my faith in the theatre as something more than the rough-and-tumble home of good fellowship and hard mumming. Every time I go I hope that I shall find once more proof that the theatre is the home of one of the great arts, the art of acted drama. Sometimes, very rarely but still sometimes, it happens, and then one can go out as a man of the theatre and look the National Gallery or the British Museum or Queen's Hall in the face.

And the faith has been conditioned always by an instinctive determination, acquired in those Birmingham-Stratford days, not to let acting go off with any homage unless it be employed to some worthy ends. I thought that Mr. Leslie Faber's performance in 'Jane Clegg,' for example, was beautiful, while I thought his performance in another play, the name of which I happily forget, was dust and ashes. I am sure he was as favourably noticed in the one as the other, but I know that he was not as good in the one as the other, and he couldn't be. Categorically, no actor can be better than his part in the part, whatever he may be, usually quite misguidedly, outside it, and when we are told that he is we may generally take it for granted that the dramatist is getting something less than his due.

In fixing this standard for ourselves as intelligent playgoers, there is one serious difficulty in the way. Much in the theatre that clearly does not comply with it is, nevertheless, extremely enjoyable. The popular entertainments provided by the one-man shows, the football fields and the prize rings — we might add the cinemas, but of them I have something to say later — may be asked to keep to their proper place and use, with our support and thanks. But if we warn them off the theatre and then patronise them when they come in, where are we? And this is continually happening. Take, as examples, two very successful plays produced in 1926, 'The Ringer' and 'The Ghost Train.' Clearly there is no National Gallery stuff about these, and yet I confess to having thoroughly enjoyed both of them. I will go further and say that I should think there was something the matter with anyone who didn't enjoy them. As works of art they do not claim to exist. They mean nothing, and they don't remain in the memory ten minutes after we have left the theatre. Unless we recall them for some purposes of argument, as I am doing now, it is unlikely that we shall ever think of them again. It won't do to dismiss them as rubbish; they are, in fact, far less rubbish than many much more pretentious plays. But they by no means can be fitted into the theatre of the imagination. They are diversions, as plainly as those that we have asked to step outside. Diversions, we say, are admirable, but this is not the place for them. And then we go to this place and applaud them when they have taken possession. This is no splitting of hairs, because they have now taken control of the very resources that we want for our own purposes, including the actors. Mr. Faber, for example, is at the time of writing in 'The Ringer.' His bad part to which I referred was in a play that challenged comparison with 'Jane Clegg' and did so quite unsuccessfully. But 'The Ringer' does not challenge such comparison at all. It is no more in the same class as 'Jane Clegg' than my boot, a tolerably good one, is in the same class as The Londonderry Air. I can't get on without my boot, and I can get on without The Londonderry Air if I have to, but that doesn't make my boot more important, even to me, than the tune. So, we can't get on without our diversions, and we can somehow get on without the imagination, but that again doesn't mean that 'The Ringer' is more important than, or even within measurable distance of being as important as 'Jane Clegg.' Nevertheless, we enjoy 'The Ringer,' and in so far as we support it we conspire to let it oust 'Jane Clegg' from the theatre. Let us see where this takes us to.

Mr. Faber, to follow the same instance, achieves an astonishing *tour de force* in 'The Ringer.' The play is also admirably produced, that is to say Mr. Faber, in the leading part, subordinates his own success to the general effect with perfect precision. The performance is, in short, altogether an extremely good one. Such a talent as Mr. Faber's obviously might be more worthily employed, but it is here by no means worthlessly employed. The play does not quicken or even touch our imagination, but it does not affront our intelligence, and it does definitely give us pleasure. But ought it to give us pleasure? Mr. Faber in a fine play braces us, and in a poor pretentious play he depresses us, but how about Mr. Faber in a play that is neither fine nor poor and pretentious? If we are going to abide by that standard of good acting exercised only in service of the best that we can find, the standard that insists on treating the theatre as the great art that it should be, what are we to say to a theatre that takes up the time of the Mr. Fabers in some other service? Ought we not to boycott it? Suppose that Mr. Augustus John were put to painting arms on railway coaches, or Mr. Kreisler to leading a super-cinema-de-luxe orchestra for moron millionaires at five hundred pounds a day. Railway coaches are of great use, and I am all for having them finely decorated, and the millionaires would no doubt derive much pleasure and satisfaction from their orchestra. But should we not protest that this was too much of a bad thing? And ought we not so to protest when 'The Ringer' comes into the theatre and press-gangs Mr. Faber and the rest?

Not, as I have pointed out, that 'The Ringer' is a bad thing, or that, in such quality, we get too much of it. Economically, Mr. Faber's answer is, of course, pat. He can't afford not to take a good thing when it is going, and if we won't pay him to play 'Jane Clegg' or 'Richard II' what is the big noise if he takes a handsome salary for playing 'The Ringer'? That is just it; we won't pay him for playing the things we most care for, and yet we will help to pay him for playing those that we like in a casual sort of way. At this point our intelligent playgoing, by which we hope to support the theatre of the imagination, seems to break down rather badly.

THE TWO THEATRES

And I do not know that there is much that we can say for ourselves in the matter. I can hear some of my readers exclaiming impatiently: 'Why trouble to say anything at all — what is all the fuss about?' Which is a comprehensible attitude to take if you are amiably bored by the inevitable difficulties of life and have no mind to add to them, but not one that makes for successful crusading. And the imagination is, as we have said, something that has to be fought for, stubbornly, even fanatically, with good old Puritan gusto. And if those of us who want a significant theatre aren't prepared to fight for it like that, the inference is that we don't really want it so passionately after all.

To some extent the inference is, however unfortunately, a just one. Our difficulty is partly one of inertia, and we may as well recognise the fact. The playgoer who is kept closely to business every day and yet wants a fine theatre can do little more to help his cause than be discriminating in the laying-out of his shilling or half-guinea. That is something, but can only be expected to show results at an evolutionary pace. The theatre will get better by those means about as rapidly as the human race is, as we are told, getting better. The impatient crusader wants quicker returns than that, and in the theatre as elsewhere he sets out to get them. But if there is any enterprise of the spirit that makes greater inroads on human energy than crusading for the theatre I have yet to discover it. It is an undertaking that requires the indefatigable drive of youth and the experience of full maturity, and the conjunction is almost unknown. Here and there a lonely fighter may survive, but the influence of single-handed endeavour cannot be more than local and temporary. During the last twenty-five years a considerable effort towards the improvement of the English theatre has been made, and with some definite result. But the result is not so signal as twenty-five years ago many people hoped it would be.

There are moments when for obscure reasons one art or another stirs with a quickened impulse in the public mind. Numbers of people up and down the country, having apparently no direct contact with each other, being indeed hardly aware of each other's existence, practise it with a new authority and yet, for all their independence, with a common inspiration. It would be an exaggeration to say that every Englishman in Elizabeth's time could write a good lyric, but an exaggeration not without point. Certainly a very large number of them could, and hardly any of them could write a bad one. In the same way, at the end of the eighteenth century and beginning of the nineteenth almost every obscure little drawing master, often far removed from any metropolitan centre of culture, could achieve exquisitely distinguished watercolour, and there was never any telling but what he might be John Sell Cotman. And about the year 1900 several little groups of people scattered about the British Isles,[1] with no central organisation and barely a speaking acquaintance with each other, were possessed of an eager desire to bring new life into the theatre. We will set down some of their names: Bernard Shaw, William Poel, William Archer, Gordon Craig, W. B. Yeats, J. M. Synge, Lady Gregory, Frank and William Fay, Miss Horniman, St. John Ervine, Lennox Robinson, Harley Granville-Barker, Iden Payne, Lewis Casson, Basil Dean, Nigel Playfair, Barry Jackson. Between the oldest and the youngest of these there is something over thirty years, but they were all actively engaged in the new movement that stirred in the British theatre during the first two decades of the present century. Encouraged by the work that they were doing, others who were dramatists but not otherwise working

[1] I should add, America. But I know less of the individual enterprises of that time there, and this is not the history of a movement but an argument based on representative aspects of a movement.

men of the theatre, took up the running, most notably among them St. John Hankin, John Galsworthy, Stanley Houghton, John Masefield, Arnold Bennett, Harold Brighouse, Allan Monkhouse.[1] Under the influence of these leaders a new dramatic vitality asserted itself in such places as Dublin, Glasgow, Manchester, Liverpool, Bristol, Birmingham and London. As the revival first gathered momentum, there was a prevalent spirit of optimism. An instinct so wide-spread and a devotion so ardent, must, it was felt, sooner or later deliver an assault that would accomplish nothing less than the reorganisation of the whole theatrical enterprise of the country. And let us see what has happened.

In isolated achievement the results have been magnificent. The records of the Abbey, the Gaiety, the Court, and the Birmingham Repertory theatres are in themselves enough to place those years securely and honourably in the history of the stage. But how much has the leaven worked among the whole? William Archer died without seeing his hope of a regenerate West End, for which he had fought so sturdily, anywhere near to being realised, and himself chiefly known at the last as the author of a brilliant and brilliantly

[1] If I do not in this connection mention such dramatists as Sir Arthur Pinero, Mr. Henry Arthur Jones and Mr. Alfred Sutro, it is from no lack of respect for their work, but merely because they seem rather to belong to another argument.

successful example of the kind of play that he had challenged for forty years. Gordon Craig has, a little perversely it may be, apparently given up the theatre in action altogether as a bad job. Miss Horniman has ceased to be an active patron, and become a reasonably impatient onlooker. Mr. William Poel, a really great man of the theatre, finds that he is not wanted, and is reduced to giving hole-and-corner performances at long intervals with wholly inadequate resources and practically no public support. The Abbey, started on its career by an array of genius such as can hardly ever have assembled at one time in a theatre, survives, but not, I gather, with unabated power, though the discovery of Mr. O'Casey is a brave new bud to its laurels. The Abbey theatre was, however, from the first, of necessity the least cosmopolitan of the influences in the new movement, and never aimed at making much impression on the British theatre at large. We have all delighted in its vigour and its lovely accomplishment, but if it has survived it has done so as a thing nobly apart. Mr. Payne has retreated into the securities of Pittsburg, Mr. Granville-Barker has, for a long intermission at least, retired from the stage that he adorned so distinctively, and shrewdly anatomises the distempers that he no longer seeks to cure in daily practice.

Mr. Nigel Playfair carries on valiantly with his

sensitive revivals, but with no very confident assurance about the future, and his productions clearly depend almost entirely on his own personality and initiative. They have hardly affected the traditions of the London stage, and if he went out of business there is no one marked out as his natural successor. Sir Barry Jackson seems to have established himself in management for as long as he cares to stay, being in the strangely unusual position to-day among managers of having money, taste, standards, and a policy. His judgment is, of course, not infallible, and he can be no surer than another man of always living up to his own standards in production, but he likes good work and understands it, and can afford to back his fancy in competition on the open market. Which incidentally means that he can afford to nurse a play in which he has faith, with what remarkable consequences he has shown on more than one occasion. Most managers, being short of either capital or faith in their choices or both, lose their nerve if a play on production does not declare itself a winner overnight. If you have no reserves, a bad opening is, in these days of monstrous rents and general ramping, unsteadying I know, but if you have no reserves you have no right to be in theatrical management with conditions as they are. And if you have no taste you are likely to be rattled by any judgment that happens to differ from your own;

but, again, if you have no taste, the sooner you fail in the theatre the better for everyone. Sir Barry Jackson has made and kept his position because he could stand fire financially and because he has refused to let his opinions be stampeded by every chatterbox who disagreed with them. Mr. Basil Dean, chiefly in association with Mr. Alec Rea, has also stayed a good course, though with a less exacting policy.[1] And largely through the agency of such managers as these and Mr. Lewis Casson, who has the advantage of being Miss Thorndike's husband, certain of the dramatists who helped to make and were part of the revival have established themselves in the theatre that has to meet the ordinary pressure of commercial competition, notably Mr. Shaw and Mr. Galsworthy.

The fact that such playwrights as these can now face all comers in the West End theatres with a reasonable chance of success is in itself evidence that the movement that began so hopefully twenty-five years ago has not been altogether without its effect on the theatre at large. We may even find that the level of the average West End play is higher — a little higher — than it was then. But when so much has been allowed, can we persuade ourselves that the revival has succeeded in creating a powerful and widely operative tradition of its own, or shows signs of doing so? I am afraid not.

[1] It is said that he is going over to cinema direction.

The theatre is as thoroughly commercialised to-day as it was in 1900, and in some respects, it would seem, more desperately so. The effort towards betterment has been and remains spasmodic, dependent on the gallantry and vision of a few individuals who have scored their successes in spite of vested interests that continue neither to know nor to care what the theatre of the imagination is. The managers of to-day who have to fight the conditions of the West End do sometimes take a risk on what they feel to be a fine piece of work, but in this we are no better off than we were in the days of the actor-manager, while in other economic respects we are worse off. Sir Barry Jackson and those two or three others apart, there is scarcely one who can consistently be relied on to encourage the good thing whatever may happen — to show that he is aware of the new life that, in spite of all disappointments, has informed our native drama in this generation. This is not said reproachfully; it is a mere statement of fact. But while it is easy to explain why the commercialisation of the theatre has, far from being stemmed, increased in our time, it is futile to pretend that it is not so. If the few men who have carried the fresh influence into the open field of competition withdrew their personal energy from their work, they would not leave a direct tradition behind them that would last a year. I say direct, because good work obviously is never wasted either at the time or when it may seem to have been forgotten. Nor am I complaining that the intelligent theatre is in a state of dissolution. The relatively few people who want such a theatre, people most of them who have at least taken an active interest as playgoers in the movement of which I have been speaking, can find in London alone a fairly constant supply of productions amply worth their attention. But the hope that the theatre as a whole might be reformed has not been realised. The crusaders have not occupied the promised land. They are not broken-hearted about it, and their example endures. The dream was, in any case, perhaps, a fantastic one. Organise the theatre, said Matthew Arnold, whose intelligence was as acute as any that has been brought to the service of the imagination in modern England. It sounded simple enough, but all the experience of the past twenty-five years has gone to show that the theatre in this country cannot be organised, by the intelligence or otherwise. When the impulse towards a new dramatic life stirs, a few men will set their mark on the time and go their way, and the great business of the theatre in general will be left to exploiters who do not know good work from bad. It is consoling to observe that even they are incapable of organising their own affairs. There is no more pleasing spectacle than that of a theatrical speculator on the rocks, and it is one with which we are frequently provided. The crusaders may be on the rocks too, but they have laid up other treasure, and still know a hawk from a hernshaw.

So far as this admission goes, then, we may have to confess that we have not been willing to fight hard enough for what we wanted in the theatre. To take a concrete instance, I hear it sometimes lodged as a complaint against Mr. Granville-Barker that he has deserted a cause of which he was one of the most effective instruments. That his ideals have suffered no diminishment is plain from all that he has written since he left the theatre, but it is urged that this is not enough, that he ought never to have left the theatre at all. I think, in the first place, that there is in this some impertinence. A man of Mr. Granville-Barker's intelligence is likely to be the best judge of his own proper calling, and in any case, as I have pointed out, the kind of energy that is worth anything in the theatre of the imagination is apt to be grudging about the daily exactions of practical stage work when middle age comes on. It probably wants to devote itself, and quite properly, to more personal designs. Mr. Granville-Barker is one of our most considerable dramatists; also he is a very slow worker. And if, after some years in the theatre as a producer, he decides that he wants to attend to his own creative purposes, I don't know who is to dispute his right to do so. But, these considerations apart, the case of Mr. Granville-Barker is instructive. There is no man of our own time who has shown a more passionate love for the theatre as a great art. And it has never been a doctrinaire love. He has not, like Mr. Gordon Craig, for example, seen a perfect vision and refrained from what he conceived to be an impossible pursuit. He has tackled the problem with his coat off in terms of the theatre as it is. His days at the Court, the Kingsway, and the Savoy, were days of hard-working trial and error, and no theoretical nonsense. He was, in short, a practical man of the theatre, who could convince everyone from the star actor to the call-boy that he knew their jobs as well as his own. He never complained that things were not other than they were; he used all his powers to exploit what was in the service of the theatre that he desired. And then he abandoned the quest. In the midst of the crusade he rode away without a word into seclusion.

Which means that he did not think it was worth it. His decision was, we may allow, a just one, but it was significant. If the cause to which he belonged had been marked out for real fulfilment, by the time he withdrew from the contest he would have been established in some authoritative position in the English theatre. And he had no effective authority. He had the deep respect of everyone who cared a cent about the dramatic welfare of this country, but he knew that he was as far from commanding the coöperation of the theatre as a whole when he ended as when he began. He was content, reluctantly perhaps, that his effort, too, should be spasmodic. He had cared up to a far point for reforming the conditions of the theatre, but it was a point beyond which he was not prepared to go. To quarrel with his view is absurd. But the average playgoer who cannot do all he would like to in behalf of his own ambitions may well be excused by the example of a man of such capacity and such unquestionable good faith.

THE PROVINCES

THESE foregoing considerations apply, it will be seen, chiefly or wholly to the London theatre. Dublin, Manchester, Liverpool, and Birmingham have shown that London is not our dramatic empire, but London obviously is and will remain by far the most powerful centre of professional theatrical enterprise. To say that the future of the drama lies with the provinces, or with amateur or community players, is a pretty figure of speech for established actors to use when speaking on tour to Rotary Clubs and High Schools, but it is no more. It is not claiming too much for my own work in the provincial repertory movement to say that at least it may be taken to have taught me the value of that work in the civic life of any place where it has taken root. Sir Barry Jackson's theatre is more important to Birmingham than all the activities of London can ever be, and the Birmingham playgoer may very well be content to let London stew in its own juice. Man for man, Birmingham may even have the laugh of London, but in the economics of art London has so many more men, so many more in effect than the seven or ten to one that the census shows. And it is no use pretending that the cumulative energy of London has no more influence on British drama than the energy of Hull, which happens at this moment to be fostering one of the most hopeful little theatre enterprises in the country. So that the state of the London theatre is the criterion by which chiefly the health of dramatic art in the country must be tested. In looking with admiration to the good work done elsewhere we have to remember that each year a very important amount of good work is done in London also, and this apart from the play-producing societies that are not in competition with the commercial theatre. If one could take a bird's-eye view of the London theatre, it would doubtless present a very unbecoming appearance, but closer investigation will at any time discover a great deal to redeem the general impression. That any considerable proportion of the sixty London playhouses will ever be devoted to dramatic art of any consequence we may now take to be more than improbable, but we may reasonably hope that a few intrepid managers will remain to see that the devotees of the imaginative theatre are not altogether starved.

And yet the work carried on outside London requires separate consideration. There is an effective reason why it cannot be said to have the future of British drama in its keeping, but the future of provincial playgoing can be and is being immensely influenced by it. The reason of which I speak is chiefly economic. The future of British drama clearly lies with the dramatists. Some of the best dramatists in the new movement have received most valuable encouragement from provincial organisations, by whom some of their best plays have first been produced. But a dramatist has to earn his living, and if he is to do so as a dramatist, it means in England that he must sooner or later get a footing with the London theatres and the touring companies that they send out. Mr. Shaw and Mr. Galsworthy have been favourite authors in the repertory theatres from the first, but the revenue that they have drawn from these theatres year in and year out would hardly keep them in boot leather. Which means that the repertory and community theatres are dependent on authors whom they cannot support, authors who have to earn their living in London,[1] or look on playwriting as a luxury rarely to be afforded. When the repertory theatres first began to establish themselves, there was a hope that in time there might be a chain of them with a coöperative policy, whereby a dramatist might look for a thirty- or forty-weeks run on the first production of a play, and prospects of regular revival. But the scheme has come to nothing, and the present economic position of the repertory theatres makes it manifest nonsense to say that the future of British drama is in their hands. The past of the British drama may

[1] Again, one should add — and America.

to a large extent be said so to be, and it is a happy thing for provincial playgoers that it is. Also these theatres will continue to find from time to time notable plays that cannot get a hearing elsewhere, but every such play means a dramatist who has got to earn his living, which his first and often generous sponsors cannot enable him to do. It is a fact that many plays of some merit and much promise have been produced by the repertory theatres, written by men who might very well have matured into fertile and important dramatists if these theatres could have offered them a career. Instead of which they have dwindled into sterility, or run to a prolixity that brings the professional play-readers to desperation. No; plainly if the future dramatists of England had to depend on the repertory theatres, they would change their job or starve. And it must be borne in mind that a nation's drama is primarily the product not of men who at some time bring off a likely or even a satisfactory play, but of men whose output as playwrights is ample and sustained.

There is another respect in which the intelligent theatres of the provinces are up against economic disabilities. They cannot regularly afford to employ really expert actors. As training schools for young players they are invaluable; indeed, by far the best to be found in the country. Many of the finest players on the English stage to-day have come from this stock, and show a breadth and intelligence in their work that they could not have hoped to acquire elsewhere. But it is the common experience of the repertory theatres that as soon as a player begins to make his mark he is tempted away by the more lavish inducements of London. Economically I think he is, in fact, often very foolish to be so tempted, but if you are earning five pounds a week and are offered ten it needs what must seem a foolhardy courage to refuse it. It is hard to believe that although your engagement may only last a few weeks you will have any difficulty in getting others as good after so auspicious a promotion, and the ten pounds is naturally accepted in nineteen cases out of twenty. Economically, as I say, the gain is often illusive, and artistically there is a clear loss. Many ten-pound-a-week players in London who drift about from one half-wit part to another would be better off in every way playing a fine repertory of parts at a fixed salary of two hundred and fifty a year. There is, however, one perfectly sound reason why the rising repertory player wants to make a move. In most of the repertory theatres the audience is not large enough to carry a play for more than a week, and in hardly any of them for more than a fortnight. With the small companies that resources will allow, each member must expect to be called upon for almost every play. The result is that after three or four seasons the strain upon a player's energies is very severe, and my own opinion is that in present conditions no one can hope to work for more than five years at most in a provincial repertory theatre without becoming seriously exhausted. And for players beyond the first buoyancy of youth, five years is an excessive period.

The consequence is that the repertory productions are generally of a not very high standard. They are admirable if due allowance is made for the difficulties, but playgoers have a right to say that they ought not to be asked to make allowances. In the early days of a new venture patience may reasonably be demanded of the audience, but after a time it wants to be assured of an expertness that shall at least be equal to that shown in the commercial theatre over the way. And it is just then, after a time, when the company is finding its form, that the dissolution usually begins. I remember W. B. Yeats once saying to me that in the London theatres you commonly saw first-rate efficiency devoted to the service of fourth-rate material. It is true that the average technical efficiency among London actors is extremely high — higher than on any other stage with which I am acquainted — though in the matter of direction or production we compare unfavourably on the whole with New York. It is true also that this efficiency spends most of its time in bolstering up work that far from being worth all that trouble isn't worth any trouble at all. In the repertory theatres the standard in choice of plays is mostly good, and sometimes extremely fine — as it was at the Gaiety theatre in Manchester and as it has always been at Dublin and Birmingham. But that there has been in any one of them a consistently first-rate level of executive skill, or anything like it, not their best friends could claim. In most of the repertory theatres that have been able to carry on for more than a precarious year or two there have been periods when the company has risen to unwonted heights, and then we have been able to see as we hardly can elsewhere what really first-class team work can be. I remember performances of 'Riders to the Sea' by the Irish Players, of 'Strife,' and 'Measure for Measure,' before mentioned, both by the Gaiety people, and one or two productions at the Birmingham Repertory theatre, when the respective companies were at the top of their powers, that remain among my very few impressions of perfection, or something near enough to perfection, in the theatre. But the economic and other strains being what they are, this form is never maintained for more than a season or so, and it has to be admitted that if you took a hundred representative repertory productions of fine plays old and new during the past twenty-five years, not more than ten of them have been half as well done as they would have been if anyone had chosen to do them in the ordinary way of business in the commercial theatres. No reproach, it need hardly be said, is implied in this plain statement of fact. The provincial repertory movement has been and remains of infinitely more significance to its own audiences than the commercial theatre has been to the audiences of London. The point is that these provincial audiences with their enviable opportunities of seeing a constant succession of good plays do not often enjoy the advantage also of seeing those plays done in a way that realises something like the full measure of their possibilities. These reflections apply inevitably with even greater force to the amateur play-producing societies that keep a high standard in their selection of plays. These societies, and particularly the village and community players, are doing valuable and often impressive work all over the country. Again, it is, I think, an excess of natural enthusiasm to say that it is here that we must look for the regeneration of the drama, but it is not too fanciful to believe that here we may find the deepest repercussion of such regeneration of the drama as there has been. But we help no one by exaggerating the present achievement. The village player is doing a very wholesome thing for himself and the community, but he is not yet a match for the village wheelwright. It is not conceivable that at present he could be, but it makes for clear thinking and progress to remember that he is not.

With these reservations we have in the provincial repertory theatres and their subsidiary ventures, if we may call them so, an inestimable privilege for the playgoers to whom they are accessible. I use Birmingham again as an illustration because I know more of that enterprise than of the others, although I have not been formally associated with it since 1919. There are living in Birmingham to-day many citizens who in the past fifteen years have seen some two hundred plays, drawn from all ages and countries, and none[1] of them unworthy to be presented in a theatre that respects the imagination. I have no analysis of the work since 1924 by me, but up to that date the following plays among others had been given: examples of the mediæval morality and mystery plays and of the Greek theatre; seventeen plays by Shakespeare, and four by other Elizabethans; six by Goldsmith and Sheridan; four by Molière; plays by Calderon, Griboyedov, Dumas, and Zola; six plays by Ibsen, plays by Björnson and Strindberg and some fifteen by other modern continental dramatists; representative works from the Restoration and Victorian drama; verse plays by such contemporary poets as Yeats, Masefield, Abercrombie and Bottomley; three plays by Synge, twelve by

[1] None? Shall we say not more than two per cent for safety.

Shaw, eight by St. John Hankin, four by Wilde, five by Galsworthy and over seventy by other modern British dramatists who have aimed at making some imaginative contribution to the theatre of their time. The effect of such work upon the civic life of a community can, I think, hardly be overestimated, even though the skill displayed in its presentation has been capricious. And there are in fact many people in Birmingham for whose lives it has opened up new horizons with who shall say what unacknowledged influence upon the character of the community as a whole. When I was at the theatre and not playing myself, I used to go into the foyer during the intervals on Saturday nights, when we produced our plays. And the scene there was one never to be forgotten. Clerks, artisans, school teachers, university professors, art students, Brummagem merchants, lawyers and parsons, railway porters and candlestick-makers, gesticulated at each other, shook each other by the lapels of the coat, stormed and persuaded on the merits and defects of this latest effort of their theatre. It was a brave thing to see the citizens of a great manufacturing town moved to as great a passion of argument by an artistic enterprise as ever they could be on the political hustings. We might not always be doing our work with positive distinction, but it was good work and it was provoking the people to a vivid exercise of the imagination. There was no lethargy in this play-going. I have seen the auditorium at the end of a performance when you might have mistaken it for the Aston Villa football ground when a goal had been scored by the home team in a cup-tie.

These repertory productions have one recommendation even when they are not very highly tuned; the play is the first consideration of whatever ability there is to command. You never see in them a player being shown off in disregard of a general unity. Plays are not there exploited for the purposes of acting, but acting is directed to the balanced presentation of plays. Miss Horniman once said that she would like to have written up at the doors of her theatre, 'The Dramatist Is Master Here.' That is the spirit in which with hardly an exception the repertory theatres of the new movement have been run, greatly to their honour. It need hardly be repeated that in these conditions the importance of the actor is in no way diminished; it is, indeed, only in these conditions that he can realise the full dignity of his calling.

The repertory playgoers have, then, on the whole, had a somewhat poor standard of acting placed before them, and have by circumstances been constrained to accept it. I mean poor when no allowances are made, poor by comparison with the best that can be seen, and I say on the whole, remembering those brief periods when a company for some reason shows a quality strikingly beyond its normal range. These playgoers, on the other hand, have been steadily trained in a realisation of what the true aim of acting should be. When they see a great play moderately well performed, the limitation is one of general skill, not of hopelessly ill-conceived proportion. It is as though a photographic negative had been under-developed; in the print there is a faintness of definition, but the image is all there, and careful scrutiny may be rewarded by a fair idea of the original. But in productions where the proper aims of acting are overlooked, it is as though an odd spot or two on the negative were sharply defined and the rest fogged out altogether. I remember, for example, a production that we did in Birmingham of 'The Merry Wives of Windsor.' It was not a good production, lacking crispness and having as it happened at that time little individual distinction in the playing or producing.[1] But it was genuinely a production of 'The Merry Wives of Windsor.' The acting, such as it was, held throughout the cast to the fixed intention of doing all it could to present Shakespeare's play. A playgoer who had never heard of Shakespeare would, with a little penetration, have been able to form a rather dim but essentially faithful impression of the great comedy. In the production of 'Romeo and Juliet' of which

[1] I was myself the producer; we did much better with the play later.

I have spoken, there were individual moments of acting far beyond the scope of any player in 'The Merry Wives of Windsor' at the time. But a playgoer not knowing Shakespeare could have formed no impression at all of 'Romeo and Juliet' as an organic creation from the production cited.

So that we look chiefly to the repertory theatres for sound employment of acting, though not at present, for economic reasons, for a high positive standard of acting ability. The simple explanation of this right instinct is to be found in the habitual choice of good plays. When an actor week in and week out has to apply his mind to fine material he falls inevitably into the way of submitting to the discipline of his authors. When, on the other hand, he is called upon continually to apply his art to insincere and devitalised material, he has no alternative but to build outside and away from his parts, supplying as he can by his own invention the life that is missing from the play. And too often it happens that when he unexpectedly finds himself acting in a play of merit and imagination, he automatically persists in bad habits that have been imposed on him by necessity. It is notorious that some very accomplished actors are so acutely aware of this difficulty that they are afraid of imaginative plays that ask for this surrender of acting skill to the dramatist's mind. It is often not so much distaste for significant work in itself as fear of the demands that it will make that keeps many of our ablest players steadily to the beaten path of mediocrity. Habits in acting technique settle very rapidly, and nothing is more disconcerting to fixed habits than ideas.

THE NATIONAL THEATRE

Obviously the ideal to be desired is a repertory theatre, or a series of repertory theatres, working to their present standard in the matter of plays, and strong enough economically to give constant employment to the best and most experienced actors who now spend most of their time in the commercial theatre. That the provincial theatres will ever be in a position to do this there are, so far as I can see, no indications. They lead for the most part a hand to mouth existence, unless they compromise in their policy, in which case they generally forfeit the esteem of the intelligent playgoer, momentarily attract a more general audience only to be found wanting when compared with the commercial theatres, and end up by pleasing nobody. Ever since I can remember there has been a desultory campaign going on with the purpose of founding a national theatre in London which should treat the drama with respect and financially be able to command the finest talent in its service. I see no evidence that the scheme is one whit nearer realisation to-day than it was twenty-five years ago. There is, I think, not the remotest possibility of raising the necessary million pounds or whatever it is by public subscription. The appeal for a few thousands to rebuild Sadlers Wells, backed by every kind of influence in and out of the theatre, having the strongest possible recommendation in being for what is virtually an extension of the invaluable work of the Old Vic, and conducted by an indefatigable enthusiast,[1] has in two years resulted in a fund that would pay about six months' interest on the proposed national endowment. People simply will not give for these purposes in England on the scale indicated by the national theatre scheme. They will, in a popular sense, hardly give at all. The only public hope of getting the money is to find a man with five millions who wants the theatre enough to part with one of them. But the rich are not, so far as I know, more open-handed in such causes than their fellows who are hard enough put to it to make ends meet. Mr. St. John Ervine and I once addressed a meeting of wealthy people on behalf — I think it was — of the Old Vic itself. It may be that we said the wrong things, but the fact remains that the audience had assembled presumably for the express purpose of being asked to pay up, and that at the end of the meeting three pounds six shillings and some pence were placed in the hat and one reckless Mæcenas made a contingent promise of twenty-five pounds.

There remains the possibility of some government that wants to extinguish itself doing so by

[1] Mr. R. P. P. Rowe.

proposing a state endowment. But governments are seldom conspicuous for such a propensity, and we and the British drama may well enough all be dead together before that happens. For myself, however, I have long since ceased to believe that a national theatre in London would serve any good purpose if we could get it. The theatrical profession in this country is not in a condition to run such a theatre if it were provided, and there is no apparent prospect of it being so. The present generation of established actors would never begin to agree among themselves as to who ought to be in control of such an enterprise, and I do not believe that a new generation, even if it were bred up in the shadow of the national theatre in being, would be any nearer to solving the problem. Moreover, London is not England — or Great Britain — and a national theatre ought to minister to the needs of Newcastle and Belfast no less than to those of the capital, the more emphatically so if it is to be anything but a private gift to the nation, that is to say if it is to be supported by public money. If a substantial fund can be raised with which to endow repertory and community enterprises all over the country, we shall see an impetus given to a real national theatre, but any attempt to focus the movement in a London building would, I am convinced, be disastrous. I am speaking of our theatrical life as it is, and as by all showing it is likely to develop. If we were another kind of people, and if conditions were what they are not, a great theatre of a national or universal character in London might be practicable. It is not a case of not wanting it. I can make such a theatre in my dreams that would be as the Promised Land to me as a playgoer. But we have learnt, in the past twenty-five years, that nothing is more unprofitable in the theatre than to let dreams run away with you. The only man who is of any use in the theatre is the practical man, the man who builds faithfully to his own vision upon conditions as they are. Once you get your project out of scale and persist in your error, you are lost. The people who have done something worth while towards organizing the theatre of the imagination are they who, after some experiment, have seen just how much theatrical activity, both before and behind the footlights, was capable of being so organised. In that work there is still ample scope for all the devotion that cares to declare itself. Let us add Sadlers Wells to the Old Vic, and half a dozen other institutions like it if we can; let us help every community of, say, a hundred thousand people to support its own theatre in which there shall be an enlightened policy in the choice of plays and a creditable standard of acting; let us see to it if it be possible that such enterprises as the Lyric Theatre at Hammersmith and the Everyman at Hampstead are not plagued by financial instability; let us even join in making a worthy festival house at Stratford-upon-Avon, where pilgrims can meet in Shakespeare's name among the enchantments of the English countryside at its loveliest; but do not let us deceive ourselves into believing that a million pound establishment in London erected in the name of imaginative drama and calling itself The National Theatre would be anything but hopelessly out of scale. The pity that it would be so cannot be lessened by pretending that it wouldn't.

The sum of it all is, so far as the actor is concerned, that generally speaking while he is regularly employed on fine drama he does not know enough about his job to do the work full justice, and that when he has learnt enough he cannot afford, or thinks he cannot, which amounts to the same thing, to turn a deaf ear to the blandishments of the theatre where fine drama is firmly put in its place, which is assumed to be outside.

THE CRUSADE

It is small wonder, indeed, that with these confused intentions among the players, producers, managers, and even dramatists, since they too are never quite sure as to which theatre they really are working for, the poor playgoer finds himself hard put to it to keep a level judgment about his adventures. Admitted that he seriously prefers good plays to shoddy ones, and that his completely satisfactory evening is when he can see what he knows is a fine play acted with high technical skill and something like complete understanding. But suppose that he has to choose between a fine play earnestly but indifferently acted and an indifferent play brilliantly acted, what is he to do then? It is a question that he often has to ask himself. I may say, having the average repertory standard in mind and not the massacre of masterpieces, the fine play for me every time, but if you decide to put your money on what is relatively first-rate acting, how am I to convince you that you are helping to make bad worse? I may say that Mr. ——, who gives so good a performance in your play would give a very much better one in mine, but you can retort that there is nobody in my play who does his job half as well as Mr. —— does in yours. I may proceed that I would far rather have to make allowance for the acting than for the play-writing, and you reply that if you come with me you find yourself wanting the production to be better while at your own choice you are content with the thing as it is, and that after some years of campaigning in the pit or the stalls you prefer letting the actors turn the dramatist out altogether to having to do half their work for them in order to keep the dramatist in. I may think all this very lazy and immoral in you, but I am conscious that my case does not make as good an effect as it should. If only I had your service in my theatre, if only the imagination had somehow put up a stiffer fight against the commercialism that you are accepting, if only the crusade had prospered a little more, then I could have shown you. You know as well as I do that I am right and you are wrong, but I could tell you so with much more point if only I were right a little more efficiently. My consolation is that as the year goes round occasions duly come along when, after all, we may go together and see the fine things finely done. To tell you the truth, I don't want to go to my theatre of the imagination so very often. I want my easy entertainment like you, and I'm for 'The Ringer' or 'The Ghost Train' with you when you like. If you don't want to join me in my repertory excursion, all right, but let me remind you that within the last year or two you have been with me to see 'Heartbreak House,' 'Back to Methuselah' and 'Saint Joan'; 'Old English' and 'Escape'; 'Rosmersholm' and 'Hamlet' at the Kingsway; 'The Way of the World' at Hammersmith; 'Trelawny of the Wells' in the Globe revival; 'Our Betters'; 'Jane Clegg'; 'The Lost Leader'; 'Juno and the Paycock'; 'And so to Bed,' and 'The Queen was in the Parlour.' All of these are plays of quality, and the productions were on the whole representative of the best that our stage can do. To these I should more doubtfully add 'The Truth about Blayds,' which did not quite fulfil the expectations of an entirely admirable first act; 'Outward Bound,' which I find seemed better at the time than it does in retrospect, good as that is; 'R.U.R.,' which was a little too sensational to be really significant; 'The Cenci,' which always strikes me as being not a great play, but the *tour de force* of a great poet; 'The Sister's Tragedy,' a thing of lovely sensibility, but not deft enough in treatment to make its full effect on the stage; 'The Madras House,' the revival of which somehow disappointed me, my expectations being what Mr. Granville-Barker had taught them to be; 'Rain,' which excited without satisfying me; 'The White Witch,' a play, as it seemed to me, of engaging interest, but one in which a few obvious and clumsy defects attracted all the public notice that it got; 'The Likes of Her,' charming in character, but rather lacking in stamina; 'They Knew What They Wanted,' where the strain on our credulity a little mitigated our pleasure in the wit and observation, and 'The First Year,' which is only a few sentimental inches off being a first-rate comedy. It is impossible to retain a critical judgment of a play that has run for twelve hundred performances, and, although I was instrumental in its first production, I don't know how good 'The Farmer's Wife' is: I only know that it still makes me laugh very much. Most people would, I suppose, by the standards I am using, include 'Hassan' and 'The Constant Nymph,' but with all my admiration for Flecker as a poet I am a heretic about the former, and 'The Constant Nymph' I enjoyed as a superb piece of showmanship, for which the dramatist was largely responsible, but not as a play. Reputed men of genius who do nothing to justify the character but behave like half-witted bounders do not interest me on the stage or off it. The real thing is worth making sacrifices for, but why all the decencies should be thrown overboard for the convenience of Lewis Dodd was not divulged to my very sympathetic playgoing mind. There are many plays that I should no doubt want to add to my list if I had not missed them, but those I have named show that it is not so derelict a crusade after all.

THE PLAY

THESE are the considerations that I find governing my experience as a playgoer so far as acting is concerned. I propose now to ask myself what kind of attitude do I bring to bear upon the play itself when I go to the theatre. Criticism of a play is easier than criticism of acting, but it is also affected by a far greater variety of standards. I am not now speaking of the reasoned and written criticism that we get, or are supposed to get, from the expert, but the direct formation of an opinion in the theatre. Leaving mental deficients out of the reckoning, one man's opinion of acting is likely to be as reliable as another's. I would as soon take the postman's word (providing that it really was his word) as, say, Mr. Arnold Bennett's, that such or such a performance was a good one. Assuming, as I do, the postman to be a regular playgoer, his opportunities for forming standards by which to judge have probably been not less than Mr. Bennett's. If it comes to making a reasoned statement on the matter then Mr. Bennett is likely to have the advantage, but in the theatre one is as likely to form trustworthy impressions of the acting as the other. Up to a point this is true also of the play. The first thing that any play has to do is to hold the attention of the audience. If it cannot do that no constellation of virtues will save it. This is the first and inevitable test to which every play is put in the theatre, and in deciding whether or no it has been passed the postman's vote is as decisive as Mr. Bennett's. It is not a question of the audience liking the play, but of its being held by it while it is in action. Some people may go away and abuse it roundly afterwards and do the play no harm, but if any considerable number of them have been allowed to be lax in their attention during the performance, nothing can redeem it.

But beyond this point there is likely to be a profound difference in the respective attitudes of the two playgoers towards the play. Of course, our postman may be a learned postman, a scholar, conceivably a better scholar than Mr. Bennett, but he probably isn't. We will take it that delivering his letters, getting to and from his job, reading his newspapers, eating his victuals, taking the baby for a walk, and going to a football match on his Saturday off takes up most of his time, and that all he has left for the drama is an evening once a fortnight or so at the theatre. This means that his knowledge of the drama is confined to the plays that he has seen, which in time may amount to a good many. But Mr. Bennett has, or I suppose he has, a more or less intimate acquaintance with the best that has been done in drama over a period of several hundred years, since the study of literature has been an important part of his occupation. And in considering the play as a play, apart from the immediate performance of it, clearly the distinction is going to tell very heavily. Is the play holding our attention, and is it being tolerably well done — so far the audience is on common ground. But when we come to ask whether it is really an interesting play, whether it has originality, whether it is subtle in its idiom and large in its conceptions, our answer must necessarily depend to a considerable extent upon our knowledge of what the best dramatists have done hitherto. To take one simple example: we have recently heard many comedies praised for their wit that cannot for a moment survive comparison in their own kind with St. John Hankin's plays; but then their admirers are, it seems, people to whom the work of even so recent a dramatist as Hankin is wholly unknown.

And so it is that while we may listen to what anyone tells us about acting and know that there is a reasonable chance of there being something in it, we have to know our man very well before we take much notice of what he says about a play. And if we ourselves do happen to know something of the achievements of drama from Athens to Adelphi Terrace, we shall find fewer masterpieces in the theatre than our neighbour at the play who vaguely surmises that English comedy began with Mr. Noel

Coward and knows nothing of Ben Jonson except that he is dead. It is unreasonable to expect all playgoers to be students of dramatic literature, nor do we want to burden ourselves with the lumber of the past. But there is a world of difference between academic pedantry and a sense of the continuity that binds the best work of all the ages into a living whole. The intellectual snobbery which pretends that any piece of hack-work thrown off by a third-rate Elizabethan writer has more vitality than the masters of our own time can show is one thing, and a perception that so beautiful and original a work as 'The Silver Box' could never have been half the play it is but for Sheridan and Shakespeare and Euripides is quite another. And how many playgoers who enjoyed 'Juno and the Paycock' were not something duller in their zest by not divining its most honourable descent from 'The Playboy of the Western World' and Molière?

It is here that the theatre is open to the challenge that has to be met by the other arts. No one is competent to judge the paintings of Mr. Augustus John or Mr. Joseph Southall who is not familiar with characteristic examples at least of the long line of representative painters of the world. Human nature is very apt to take it for granted that the best that it knows is the best that there is, and will thus sometimes in ignorance attribute great merit to very inferior work. Many people who had never read a line of Milton, Wordsworth, or even of Tennyson who was in their midst, thought that Martin Tupper was the greatest English poet. The excited publicists who rained anathema on Mr. Epstein's 'Rima' had no ideas on sculpture that took them beyond the Albert Memorial — a work, by the way, that is at present underrated. They knew of nothing but our modern academic variations on the Greek theme, being innocent of contact with China, Persia, or Egypt. They can hardly, indeed, have looked even at the figures in our own churches, carved in the fifteenth century or so by Italianate Englishmen. The critics of Rima's hands might with advantage study the supporting angels on the Countess of Suffolk's tomb in Ewelme church. The discretion of inviting Mr. Epstein to carry out such a work as the Hudson Memorial may possibly be questioned, but the people who with souls virgin of all these contacts offered their observations in public on his art naturally succeeded only in making themselves ridiculous.

In the same way opinions of a play are of little interest unless we know them to be supported by a respectable knowledge of the general achievements of drama. Uninstructed opinion, if it comes from a naturally shrewd person, may it is true often be an indication of the immediate success or failure of a play with the public, but it is of no use whatever as a guide to permanent values, nor is it any criterion as to what we shall ourselves think of the play if our own opinion happens to be relatively instructed. It is true of drama as it is of all art that the work that lasts is that which, accepting tradition, adds significantly to it. Tradition that in one mind is a lifeless instrument is a vital source in another, and by this difference is decided whether we are given work that may take the fancy of the moment or work that is for the moment and, as the figure goes, for all time. Each generation produces playwrights who deftly supply the needs of those who in that generation have no intellectual horizons, who are aware of no continuity. A playwright takes the fashionable moods and activities of an age, and if he aspires to a reputation for originality, adds a few tags from current demagogy. Upon the tradition that he finds established in the theatre at the time he imposes a veneer of this material, and comes forward as the new dramatist. But his personal contribution is concerned only with the trivial and fugitive aspects of life and manners. He is not using these aspects as the most convenient idiom by which to express his vision of fundamental things. So far as he takes these into his survey at all, it is from the tradition that he has accepted inertly, without any galvanising touch. He relies wholly for his appeal upon the response of people who see on his stage a mirage of their external interests and behaviour. His reflection of life, such as it is, is projected upon a background of entirely conventional thought and emotion, not translated by his own imaginative experience and discovery. This is the kind of lifeless realism that has given that form a bad name. Skilfully contrived it is often very successful by the tests of the box office. Mankind always enjoys seeing reflections of itself, even though they reveal nothing. But in work of this character tradition has merely been exploited for paltry uses. It has been dignified by no organic process. I do not know that any particular harm has been done. Responsible art goes its way unaffected by these employments. But nothing durable has been added to the records. Spectators who in the theatre have no perspectives either historical or spiritual, are enthusiastic about work that will be forever forgotten by the time a new generation bestows its favours on the adroitness that in turn applies the fresh superficial idiom of the time to a tradition that it cannot quicken. I may add that my distaste for barracking the player while the game is on disinclines me to give what I take to be perfectly obvious contemporary examples of my meaning.

The other kind of playwright sets about his business in quite another way. He, too, may use the idiom of his own time, but he never uses it for its own sake. He is likely also, though by no means certain, to use the tradition of the theatre more or less as he finds it. If we consider the technical methods of three of the most important dramatists of the past thirty years, Sir Arthur Pinero, Mr. Shaw, and Mr. Galsworthy, we shall observe instructive distinctions. When Mr. Shaw, and a little later Mr. Galsworthy, came effectively into the theatre, the English stage was primarily dominated by a technical tradition of which Sir Arthur Pinero was the acknowledged master. Mr. Shaw broke with this tradition decisively, modifying for his own purposes and with his own invention the traditions of older or more distant practice, those, for instance, of the English chronicle plays, and of the Russian and Scandinavian theatres. In outward shape Mr. Shaw's plays bear no more resemblance to Sir Arthur Pinero's than they do in mood and substance. Mr. Galsworthy, on the other hand, whose imaginative purpose is as far removed as Mr. Shaw's from Sir Arthur Pinero's, comes much nearer to a direct inheritance of the older dramatist's manner. As it passes through Mr. Galsworthy's hands we are aware, certainly, of important innovations, notably the use of the convention known as the fourth wall, and a subtly different view as to what is the precisely dramatic moment at which to lower the curtain. In treatment of life within this manner, in the use of detail and the kind of detail used, in conceptions of dramatic speech, in the shaping of action and in the demands made upon character, there is, as any investigation shows, as much discrepancy between the two dramatists not only as there is between either of them and Mr. Shaw, but as there is between any one of the three and Otway or Aristophanes — which difference it may be said in passing is not so comprehensive as may be supposed. Mr. Galsworthy, in taking over something of the Pineroic shape for his plays, was no less effecting an organic development of tradition than was Mr. Shaw when he went further afield for the tradition upon which his creative powers were to be exercised. The one choice was not inherently better than the other. As a purely personal opinion, I incline to the opinion that the tradition appropriated and developed by Mr. Shaw is on the whole more natural to the genius of British playwriting than that so admirably expanded by Mr. Galsworthy, which seems to derive more closely from a French influence of the eighteen eighties, and through that from our own restoration theatre, which abandoned the models by which the Elizabethans had achieved so magnificent an expression of our native genius. I need hardly say that I do not for a moment suggest that there is the least similarity of mind between Mr. Galsworthy and the dramatists who presided over the vogue of what is conveniently if not very acutely called the machine-made play. It was, indeed, partly his dissatisfaction with that kind of play that induced him to divide his attentions between the novel and the drama. Nor, I think, could any mind of our own age be found that is more richly characteristic of our native genius than that which has produced 'The Forsyte Saga,' 'Strife,' 'The Pigeon,' and 'Escape.' Finally, there is no possibility of confusing for a moment Mr. Galsworthy's dramatic technique with Sir Arthur Pinero's, but the fact remains that Mr. Galsworthy did approximately evolve his technique from the tradition that was prevalent in the theatre when he began to write, whereas Mr. Shaw did not, which is to say that the serious [1] dramatist in looking for a tradition on which to build may find it as satisfactorily here as there. It may be noted, as marking the effect that the choice has on the public, that when a dramatist uses a technique that in external shape is unfamiliar to the audience, many people at once remark that though the work may be interesting in many respects, it is, of course, not a play at all. As they have frequently said of Mr. Shaw's stage productions, but not of Mr. Galsworthy's.

Let us suppose then that the dramatist elects to use the idiom of his own time, that is to write about

[1] Serious is a word that we almost grow afraid of using, so often is it supposed to denote something heavily solemn. But we should not be intimidated in this way. Every artist who is worth the name is serious, and there's an end of it.

what we call contemporary life, and that he works along his own lines from a tradition familiar to the audiences of his time. At first glance his plays will then present an appearance not unlike those of the playwright whose vogue we have considered to be momentary, and beyond hope of recovery once it has passed. This other playwright, more worthily called the dramatist, is, we assume, doing work that will survive. When it is first produced it stands neither more nor less than the usual chance of scoring a box-office success, but whatever its luck may be then it will always retain an interest for people who think some study of the drama to be at least a useful adjunct to their playgoing. That any play, however fine it may be, will have any but a fitful hold on the stage say two hundred years after its composition, we cannot tell; whether 'Heartbreak House' and 'Strife,' for example, will be at all widely known to playgoers in the theatre of 2125. But it is certain that, whatever the state of the theatre and its drama may then be, intelligent understanding of that theatre will be to some extent influenced by a knowledge of such works as these. And what, we may ask, is it in them that will induce the repertory manager of 2125 in making out his list of revivals at least to give such plays his sympathetic consideration, and probably put them among the chosen?

'FEE FIRST'

THE answer is to be found in the fact that their authors are not, in Ruskin's phrase, fee-first men. Ruskin divided work into two classes, that which is done primarily for its own sake and that done primarily for the money that it would earn. In recognising the essential justice of this, we need not be stampeded by Ruskin into a doctrinaire idealism. We may remember that Johnson, who was as honest and as sensible a man as Ruskin, asserted that no one but a fool would write at all unless it were for money. Something of the truth lies with both sides of the argument. Nothing is easier for the man of talent than to persuade himself that he is not working because inspiration is not upon him, while the real reason is that his purse is not empty at the moment and he is lazy. But then, we must allow, good writers do often get driven by necessity beyond a reasonable rate of production, and in directions against their proper bent. It is probable that there is a natural economy in these matters that keeps the balance about level, and some men, under the pressure of anxiety have still contrived to do their gifts full credit. A writer who has really got something to say is likely to say it whether he is fancy free in the choice of his subjects or is called upon to supply a specific market. It is, I suppose, probable that if Mr. Lascelles Abercrombie had been a rich man he would never have become a professor of English and that we should not have had from him the remarkable series of books on poetics that are the most notable contribution to English criticism since the appearance of Matthew Arnold's essays. We might then, it is true, have had more of his poetry, but the point is that under economic pressure he has produced work of the finest quality and done his great powers nothing but honour. Many distinguished books in our own time have been written on commission, and the history of literature is studded with examples of memorable works done with creditors at the door, though we need be under no illusions as to the nonsense in general about the discipline of the garret. Two conditions are necessary for this worthy production at the dictates of circumstance. First, that the writer shall truly have vision, and, second, that the employment in which he finds himself shall not make the expression of his vision wholly impossible. The painters of the Italian renaissance were engaged largely on subjects not of their own choosing, but there was nothing in the subjects to preclude a free and ample play of their individual gifts. The Waverley novels were written expressly to repair the fortunes of a bankrupt house, and in them Scott diligently adapted his talents to a popular demand. We may doubt whether the challenge of Byron would in itself have induced him to give up poetry had it not been for the grosser challenge of the bailiffs. But the constraint did not prevent him from finding in romantic prose fiction an entirely satisfactory means of self-expression.

Sometimes, nevertheless, and more than ever in these days when the spread of journalism means a huge and incessant demand for copy, good writers are tempted into engagements that they cannot keep without loss of freshness and independence. A writer who is under the daily or even weekly necessity of delivering his material to time may, if his choice of subjects is left completely to his own discretion, and if his mind is one of uncommon fertility, manage to preserve his form, but when he has to write by the occasion and not by his election, the occasions more often than not being of no interest whatever to him, he inevitably becomes garrulous and stale. The spectacle of the writer who has something to say being remorselessly driven to say something else is one of the most displeasing afforded by the calling of letters. He is the kind of fee-first man who is greatly to be pitied; but there is another kind who needs no pity, who is affably satisfied with himself and highly prosperous, and who is, if not a positive nuisance, at best a trader whose merchandise we could do very well without.

For it has to be recognised that while writing is, when finely practised, one of the great arts, it is possible for a nimble wit to acquire a certain trick of it that may be a valuable commercial asset without being of the smallest significance. And the most profitable field for the exploitation of this trick is the theatre. In London alone there are something like sixty playhouses that, in the opinion of their proprietors, have to be supplied year in and year out with plays. There is, clearly, nothing like enough intelligent playwriting to go round on this scale. A large proportion of the sixty, however, have no need for intelligent playwriting — what mostly is wanted is entertainment devised to the popular pattern of the time. The theatres are, with a few exceptions, controlled in groups by speculative finance that, as I have already pointed out, knows as little about intelligent playwriting as it does about the seventeenth-century metaphysical poets or the Einstein theory. But it does know a good deal about the popular patterns, and if it fills half a dozen theatres with plays of a fashionable cut, it can — or fondly believes it can — rely on a trading balance when the balance of profit and loss is struck. And this is precisely the type of play that can be manufactured by the trick of which I have spoken. The writer who has mastered the trick, whose preoccupation in life has been to master it, is above all sensitive to current modes, and can readily accommodate his dexterity to all their mutations. You will not catch him wasting his time on work that will not, he believes, be entirely to the satisfaction of his highly esteemed customers — he is, with assurance of his continued attention, their most obliged, most humble servant. He really does know the trick, and it is he who keeps some forty out of the sixty theatres open. Speculative finance could not do without him, and his rewards are, properly, great. Everybody thinks he is a good fellow, which he is, his friends admire him as a successful playwright, as also he is, and a few uneducated people assure themselves, and him, that he is a considerable dramatist, which he is not. For he is, in the beginning and the end, a fee-first man, and considerable artists are never that. He enjoys his work, he spares none of his ability in making it as effective as he can, he feels friendly towards it when it is done, and likes other people to do the same. In these respects he might be the genuine thing. But the invariable preliminary to his every undertaking is an exact calculation of what it will bring in. He usually sees to it that it will bring in something substantial, and that is the conclusion of the contract. He has no further claims upon us.

I would not be taken to hold that the serious artist ought to be indifferent as to the material rewards of his work. On the contrary I admire the man who, doing the utmost that he can as an artist, then proceeds to do the utmost that he can as a trader in his wares. No artist was ever yet the worse for having a spare shilling in his pocket, even though it has sometimes inclined him to loaf a little at his own or the inn fireside. One of the most encouraging aspects of our sufficiently formidable civilisation is, indeed, the fact that many of the best artists do somehow in the long run manage to hold their own pretty well in the market. The best sellers are not uncommonly the best writers. Most of our trick performers would, I suppose, in their respective mediums be put to it to match pennies with Mr. Hardy, Mr. Shaw, Mr. Galsworthy, Mr. Bennett, Mr. Wells, Mr. Masefield, Mr. Sinclair Lewis, Mr. Walpole, M. Maeterlinck, M. Pirandello, and M. Čapek. Shakespeare was probably the richest working dramatist of his time, and the big money men of later generations were Pope, Byron, Scott, Dickens, Thackeray, and Tennyson. Worthless writers were, we know, their competitors in worldly fortune, and men of superb genius such as Blake and Landor have counted their literary earnings by half-crowns. But the accountant-general of letters, if he made a summary of his ledgers, would show that on the whole the men who matter have carried on a successful financial contest with the men who don't. Fortunate as the circumstance is, still more fortunate is the circumstance that the men of signal merit are never debauched by their success. They cannot be persuaded to become fee-first men.

AND OTHERS

Mr. Shaw and Mr. Galsworthy — it is of them, it will be remembered, that we are speaking at the moment — have probably earned as much by their plays as most successful dramatists of our time; in any case they are conspicuously among those who have brought a liveliness to the box-office. They have, too, mostly used the habit of contemporary life in their plays, that is to say a habit that their audiences recognise without effort. In these respects there is nothing to distinguish them from the writers who supply the theatre that is governed by commercial consideration first and last. But Mr. Shaw and Mr. Galsworthy, with all the other dramatists who have helped to renew the vigour of the theatre during the first quarter of the present century, differ from the dexterous fashion-fanciers in that they have used the manners of their time as an image through which to advance their own vision and convictions, and they have steadily refused to allow the box-office to influence their work while it was being done. This is the claim that always provokes the people of easy artistic virtue to accusations of highbrow humbug. Mr. Shaw, they exclaim, wants his plays to succeed in the theatre as much as anyone else, and all this talk about intellectual integrity is nonsense. Of course Mr. Shaw wants his plays to succeed, and being a practical man of the theatre he uses every device that he can master in order to make them succeed, and the most popular dramatist in Europe to-day may be said to have done it pretty effectively. But his devices have not been employed merely for popular success in itself; they have been scrupulously employed towards the successful presentation of his vision on the stage. He has, indeed, desired success as keenly as any man, but he has never been willing to achieve it at the cost of disloyalty to himself. This is the truth of every dramatist who is worthy of respect as well as his fees, and it is this fixed courage that enrages the people who have none. This it is also that gives the plays, of which we have chosen 'Heartbreak House' and 'Strife' as examples, their vitality, and will keep them fresh in the interest of playgoers who cherish the theatre of the imagination and study its records.

It is too much to say that the men who write such plays would continue to be dramatists if they had no success in the theatre. For nearly two hunered years the best writers in England forsook the theatre, not because they had no dramatic gifts, but because they were not wanted in it, were indeed effectively kept out of it. I have never believed that if Byron, Shelley, Landor, Browning, Dickens, Morris, Swinburne, perhaps Wordsworth,

Coleridge and Keats, had lived in a time when fine drama was welcomed by the theatres they would not have supplied it. A writer of original powers may now and again be found who genuinely feels the theatre to be, as the late Sir Walter Raleigh was once heard to call it, a bastard art, and want to have nothing to do with it. But while a live theatre will always attract the creative genius of its time, it is also true that the drama cannot flourish if it is excluded from the theatre. If the dramatists of the modern renaissance had not found audiences they would undoubtedly have used their gifts in other forms, but it does not follow that their devotion to drama was contingent upon successful competition for the great prizes of the commercial theatre. Some of them have walked off with these, but that is a lucky accident of fortune. These dramatists made, or helped to make, a theatre for themselves, and although it has so far proved to be a theatre of relatively small financial scope, it has been vigorous enough to provide them with a sufficient reason to go on writing plays even if they do not make their impressive excursions into more affluent scenes. Or we may say, more exactly, if the dramatists of whom we are speaking had never attracted overtures at all from the vested interests of the commercial theatre, they would in all probability have expanded the resources of their own theatre to enable them to go on playwriting.

It may be that such a condition would have been for the general good of the drama, if not for some bank balances, but the speculation makes no matter. Once Mr. Shaw, for example, had begun writing plays, nothing was going to stop him, and if he had never known what a long run meant he would have contented himself with the more modest rewards of what might then have been a more effective repertory system. Short of complete exclusion from the theatre, in fact, the best dramatists of our time would have gone on writing their plays because that was the form through which they most wanted to express themselves; just as Mr. Shaw and others actually did go on writing for some years with only less than complete exclusion.

It is this test that seems to me incidentally to dispose of the cinema as a serious art. The poet, the composer, the painter, will all continue to do their work even though it should never bring them a penny of the few that they have to get in some other way to keep them from starving. The dramatist is not quite in the same case. It is essential for him to come by some little measure at least of commercial success, as otherwise he has no audience; and without an audience he functions incompletely as a dramatist. Mr. Shaw would have continued to write his plays had he never hit the fancy of the general body of playgoers, but he would hardly have done so had he been unable to get them put before any playgoers at all. With this reservation, however, the dramatist who respects his work shares with the poet and the painter and the composer a resolution to go on with it, however scanty the prospects of reward may be. But if you eliminated money considerations, and big money considerations at that, from cinema enterprise, the whole thing would have come to an end in a month. It is not conceivable that anyone would go on making moving picture scenarios merely for the purpose of satisfying his spiritual necessities. This, no doubt, will seem fantastic nonsense to any cinema pundit who may happen to read it; but it does so happen that the artists, the people who are the real foundation of any art, however commercialised it may become, are prepared to stand by their work for no other reason than that if it comes to it.

This, I am aware, may be said to be an empirical argument only, but it is none the less one which the people who claim that the cinema is threatening the life of the drama as we know it will have difficulty in answering. It is a digression, but I will attempt to show on more philosophical grounds why I do not think that the cinema can ever supersede or even importantly compete with that art of the theatre that has been evolved round the drama of the spoken word. What the possibilities of the cinema may be in the direction of light-symphonies, pattern-melodies or even such less moon-raking projects as plain choreography I have here no occasion to enquire. Further, I think the cinema provides the most engaging form of newspaper and travel-gazette, and I can see that for those who like it the skill and acrobatic energy, say, of Mr. Douglas Fairbanks, is as good an entertainment as the stock lines provided by the commercial theatre, with something to spare. For the ability shown in this kind of work by Mr. Fairbanks, Mr. Chaplin, and half a dozen others, we can have nothing but admiration. I have, I hope, said enough to show that

I do not undervalue popular entertainment, even though I do not confuse it with significant art. As popular entertainment the cinema has immense scope, and it is such men as these who are responsible for most of the work that, within those limitations, does matter. They are under no illusions as to what the real function of the cinema is, and they understand that the best way to fulfil it is to let one man, with what mechanical assistance he needs, be responsible for a picture right through from its conception to its appearance on the screen. And so they invent their own material, design their own production, and make themselves the centre of acting interest. I have watched their industry and technical resource, and know that for hard work and application they are examples that many, if not most, of the workers in the theatre might note and be ashamed. For instance, I saw Mr. Chaplin at work when he was beginning to devise his new picture about a circus. He had, in his part as a clown, to walk a tight-rope; the incident on the screen would occupy about half a minute, and for several weeks he had put in a long spell of practice daily, until he had made himself an expert performer between the poles. How many actors would, or could, do as much for a dramatist? Sir Frank Benson caused a sensation and made a name for himself as a stage athlete by climbing a property tree as Caliban and jumping over a chair as Dr.

Caius, but Mr. Fairbanks can climb up the side of a house or jump over a tin-Lizzie if he is put to it. All of which is very jolly, and does really show that if their work is not very serious, these cinema stars take it very seriously. Mr. Fairbanks, in order to keep himself fit, surrounds himself on his 'lot' with champions of international class, swimmers, pugilists, sprinters, rough-riders, high-steppers of all sorts, and asks no quarter from any of them. Not to be too precise, he is no longer a youth, and they say he can still do the hundred in evens. That may be a shade on the side of compliment, but certainly he would be no bad choice for the decathlon in any company. Good fun as this is, it is not only fun, but a rigorous and strictly observed discipline. The popular notion of Hollywood as the home of self-indulgent trifling has, indeed, no connection with facts. Man for man there is probably no harder working community in the world. And to be privileged to watch one of the big pictures in the making there, is to be amazed at the ingenuity displayed. I have seen an important 'shot' being taken with the whole establishment, actors, directors, electricians, camera men, mechanics, clerks, and casual labourers on a tip-toe of excitement as after numberless experiments some new device of Mr. Fairbanks's agile mind was at length finally transferred to the film. For myself, I never get that kind of thrill in the picture houses, but I found it there at Hollywood as surely as in a Scots regiment marching behind its pipes or a close finish to the boat-race. With which grateful and, I trust, ample concessions, let us return to the point in question.

As a serious art the moving picture does not compete with the spoken drama as acted on the stage, in the first place because its anomalies are not those that belong to a convention, but accidental and disturbing, and secondly, because it has no texture. The acted drama can never, it is true, achieve quite the purity of convention possible to the other arts, because the personality of the player is, even from performance to performance, to some extent a capricious factor. The spoken word in any play is a formal and conventionalised word, whether it be in the blank verse of Shakespeare or the so-called realistic idiom employed by Mr. Galsworthy. The effects of actual conversation are selected, heightened, arranged into dramatic sequence, coördinated. The most elaborate care may be taken, as by Tchekhov, to conceal this manipulation, but the art is none the less evident on a moment's reflection, and Baron Nikolay Tusenbach uses as highly formalised, if not as deeply significant, a speech as Macbeth. Logically, the players who utter this speech ought to be relatively conventionalised also, and it is the difficulty that arises at this point in the theatre that has set such purists as Mr. Craig and Mr. Yeats dreaming of masks and marionettes. Here, too, was Walter Raleigh's opportunity for his reproach about a bastard art. But to work in the theatre, or to be a devoted playgoer, is, as we have admitted, not to be too inflexible in our logic, and not to be too easily moved by reproaches. While, however, the theatre is no place for the doctrinaire, it still maintains a convention that its workers delight to respect. Our own time has seen a great advance in what is called natural acting. Down to the time of Irving the common method of acting, so far as we know anything about it, aimed at a formalised technique in movement and gesture that corresponded with the formalised speech of the drama. With the new influences that have brought a speech into the theatre which is apparently far less formalised, though on examination it is plainly not so, has arisen a new school of acting in which the appearance of natural behaviour is a good deal more difficult to see through than it is in the dramatist's words. Nobody could listen to a page of Mr. Galsworthy's dialogue without realising that, however perfectly contrived the illusion might be, no casual conversation in real life could ever have this conciseness, balance, and steadiness of purpose. But to watch Sir Gerald du Maurier acting is altogether more deceptive. Here, surely, the unwary spectator may say, and not so very unwary at that, is the effortless reproduction of a natural manner on the stage. A hundred little turns and flourishes of style seem to come into play at the bidding of the moment's impulse, casual glances and hesitant syllables that seem hardly intended for the audience's notice, so apparently spontaneous and fugitive are they. This is the kind of acting that makes simple people assert that it is not acting at all, that so-and-so has a part in which he merely has to be himself. But it is in reality as carefully studied and as exact in its deliberation as were the measured evolutions of the Greek tragedians or the rhetorical counterpoint of Edmund Kean and Phelps. The unsophisticated playgoer who, as he watches Sir Gerald du Maurier acting, assures himself that this is not art but nature, is probably able in daily life to get up from his chair and go out of the room without difficulty; let him try to go out of that room on the stage as he now sees it being done, and he will find that it is far from being the same thing, that to his surprise he is totally incapable, without making an exhibition of himself, of doing what it had taken an accomplished actor a very long time to learn by precise art to do, as it seems, so naturally.

But while the play and the playing, of whatever school, are thus governed by a convention, there is a small margin of accidental effect in every performance, that cannot be eliminated. An experienced actor, to fetch a far instance, would not be likely to sneeze as he was delivering Mark Anthony's oration even if he had a cold; but he might do so, and the possibility indicates crudely the margin of which I speak. On the whole, however, the margin is a negligible one, and in practice interferes little with our pleasure as playgoers. We are willing to dispense with the masks and marionettes, and to accept actors of flesh and blood who on the stage often remain physically what they are if we meet them in the street, and yet are expressing character through a medium that is conventionalised away from what we call real life. In other words, the physical presence of the actor remains the one inescapably natural thing where everything else, character, action, scenery, speech, are creations of art. So used are we to this condition of the theatre, that we probably seldom think of it as an anomaly at all, but anomaly it is. The accidents of stage-art — the sneeze, for example — are in the general run of our playgoing negligible. The anomaly of which I speak is a more important matter, but we recognise that it is incidental to the whole convention of the theatre, and a condition without which stage performance as we have known it for five hundred years could not exist.

We may even go further, though this raises a more debatable problem of æsthetics, and say that the actor's personality is an essential contribution to the art of the theatre. The purists here quarrel with the actors who, in their opinion, are apt to overestimate the value of what is called interpretation. The theory of interpretation is, indeed, responsible for many vagaries on the stage. The actor is an executant; and I hope that no actor will do me the injustice of supposing that I say this of a calling that I worship this side of idolatry, in disparagement. It is sometimes argued that a creative work of art may, and should, mean many different things to different people, that it is, in fact, susceptible of many different interpretations, each one of which may be logically vindicated. This I believe to be a fallacy. The most notorious storm-centre for this particular opinion is perhaps the part, and with it the play, of Hamlet. It is no unusual thing for the attitude towards a new actor of Hamlet to be one of speculation as to what freshness he will bring to the interpretation of the part. Argument about Hamlet is, admittedly, endless, and admittedly able critics differ in their conclusions. But the argument and differences do not mean that Shakespeare himself was not sure about what he meant when he wrote Hamlet. Unless creative purpose and achievement are to go for nothing, he knew precisely what his intention was, and if we say that he may have meant any or all of a dozen different things we either accuse him of gross inefficiency as an artist or confess ourselves to be addle-pates. We have, certainly, every right to say humbly that of so vast a conception and form we are unable to determine the exact and full significance, and in so far as this is so to be curious as to any clues that this that or the other performance may afford us. But this is not at all the same thing as saying that it is of itself a commanding merit in the part that there may be a dozen proper ways of playing it. There is only one proper way of playing Hamlet, and while we may never decide what that way is, we ought to recognise that so long as we remain in doubt we are doing less than justice to Shakespeare. The advocate of interpretation would say that it was not a question of making the best of our limitations, but a positive enrichment of experience to see twelve actors play Hamlet in twelve different ways. But the advocate of Shakespeare feels that the real enrichment would be to see twelve actors play it in the same way, and be convinced that all of them had discovered the secret. For to the riddle contained in every great work of art there may be twenty plausible answers, but there can be only one right one.

So that, in a sense, the purists have much to say for their view in this matter of the actor and interpretation. They demand that the actor shall faithfully represent, and let what interpretation there is to be done lie between the dramatist and life. But here, again, we remember that to be doctrinaire in the theatre is to entangle yourself in constraints that hamper and would in the end destroy all activity if they were not confronted by the necessities of getting on with the job. In the pure arts theory and practice can, apart from economic difficulties, be made to square easily enough. When a Keats writes an 'Ode to a Nightingale' he may in his sublime modesty feel that it is not as good as it ought to be, but he knows that if he has fallen short of perfection it is because of his own limitations and not because of the nature of poetry. But it is specifically in the nature of the theatre as we know it for practical, and what magnificent, purposes in our civilisation, that you cannot achieve in it a perfection that shall satisfy æsthetic theory. It is thus that we have to take it or leave it. The compensations are many and great, the immediacy of appeal, the force of the impact, the communal excitement, the scope of expression. But to ask for the artistic purity that we find in 'Lycidas' or Ver Meer's 'View of Delft' or the Parthenon or in a mediæval wooden Virgin,[1] is to ask for something that the theatre, as in any reasonable view we have to consider it, cannot provide. We may, therefore, allow the personality of the actor its due place as a contributor to the general effect that we as playgoers enjoy. Disregarding the poor play that is pulled through to some kind of success by skilled acting,

[1] I omit any example from music, because it is not within my purpose to discuss in that connection the question of interpretation that would again be involved.

the fact remains that, whatever devout theories we may hold, many a fine part in a fine play takes on an added interest because of some quality that a particular actor, and he alone, is able to bring to it.

THE theatre, then, for all its loose ends, submits to an artistic convention, which means that in the theatre we do get life translated into terms of art, and such imperfections as exist there arise from the nature of the convention and do not gravely impair its power. The concessions we have to make are slight, and it is possible for the playgoer who really loves the arts and keeps habitually in contact with their finest expression to watch a play and be spiritually invigorated. The life on the stage crystallises into some coherent artistic shape before him, and he is undisturbed by having to give a little for the much that he takes. In the cinema, however, we find ourselves in another world altogether, and it is a world in which conditions of art do not prevail at all. I am speaking now, it must be remembered, of the moving picture as an art comparable to that of the theatre, not as a popular entertainment. The anomalies that now face us are not the incidental defects of a convention that is on the whole acceptable, but distractions pervading a method of expression that does not realise what the function of convention in art is, or even that a convention is necessary. And this, I believe, is not due to the fact that the moving picture is as yet only in its infancy, but to an inherent disability of the form. The unit of the screen life is a moving photograph of a human being bereft of speech. A photograph, even a moving photograph, may be an interesting thing, but it cannot be an artistically significant thing, because in so far as it is anything, it is a literal reproduction of a natural object deprived of those dimensional aspects that make it susceptible to an art convention on the stage. That the object photographed is acting does not alter the case. To see Mr. Henry Ainley acting Macbeth and to see a moving photograph of him acting Macbeth are experiences different not in degree but in kind. The actor's place in the theatre is justified in preference to the marionette of the purists by the fact that he establishes contact with the audience by his living presence, which does physically communicate life and evoke that response which is not only the delight of the audience to show but also a vital element without which the art of the theatre is essentially incomplete. To take away from that living presence its dimensional aspect, is literally to make it no longer living or a presence, and to rob it of that power of communication by which the whole contract is finally given its artistic validity. I have never for a moment felt in watching the screen that the living presence was before me, and I have never for a moment known the response that the presence, and the presence only, induces. To impute this statement to prejudice would be absurd. What conceivable reason for prejudice could there be? I merely record my experience, and it is an experience that can be accounted for by fundamental æsthetic necessities. When the screen is showing something that professes no concern with art, the limitation is of little consequence, just as one cares nothing for style or character or truth when one is enjoying a detective story. But when this concern is professed, the disqualification seems to me to be absolute. The theatre takes its place, with some difficulty, as a great art, by virtue of a condition that the moving picture inevitably nullifies. So far as the drama in which men and women are the medium is concerned the cinema is not, and never can be, in serious competition with the theatre of the imagination.

The difficulty is not one of this dimensional aspect only. The absence of speech is an inhibition no less crippling. If the theatre accepts the actor — the natural man of limbs and features in a world of convention — and adapts, as it has adapted, its drama to this acceptance, clearly the means of communication proper to the actor, speech, is a necessity not only of expedience but of art as it has there accommodated itself. On the screen, when the same natural man is the medium still, his inarticulateness is grotesque. Not being a man, but the photograph of a man, it is true that we could hardly expect him to speak, but the silence of these figures that are so manifestly not images wrought by an artist but shadows of reality divested even of their original virtue, adds to the futility of the pretence. And if, as is proposed, a synchronisation of the spoken word with screen movement should be introduced, we should, it may be presumed, have reached the limits of confusion to which people who trifle with the arts can reduce themselves.

SECONDLY, though this is perhaps no more than a variation on the same theme, the impression made by any art is subtly dependent upon a consciousness in the spectator of a texture that has been masterfully employed by the artist, and the cinema provides no such texture for the artist to employ. The writing of a scenario is, doubtless, a very difficult thing to do well, but so is making an umbrella or running a hotel. No one can pretend that such action and dialogue as are required by the scenario itself are capable of affording anything like ample satisfaction to a creative mood. When the dramatist has finished a play, it needs stage performance to realise to the full its potential life, but it is already an organic whole before it is acted, even though acting will expand its functions. Mr. Shaw can print a play and find an eager public for it before it is put on the stage, and be assured that his standing as an artist will not be prejudiced in consequence. The measure that thinking people throughout the world have taken of Shakespeare is, on the whole, an adequate one, but it is founded far more on the reading of his plays than on experience of them in the theatre. But clearly no scenario writer would be so witless as to submit his work to this test. As it leaves his hands it has no independent life, it has no resemblance to an organic whole. So that up to this point there is no question of that final mastery of texture which is a condition of art. The director who takes over the scenario is in no better case. His material consists of the actors and the general machinery of production, but he is using these not to express any conception of his own; he is using them to supplement the unrealised conception of the scenario writer. The director's work is, again, as difficult as the most ingenious talent could desire, but it is a confusion of terms to speak of it as creative. He manipulates material, he does not in any profound sense shape it. It would be as reasonable to apply the term of creative artist to Napoleon because he was a superb strategist, or to the cook because he knows his ingredients to a nicety. Producing, or directing, is a highly skilled business, demanding many qualities of intelligence and taste, but it is specifically not a creative art and nothing is gained by pretending that it is. In the case of men like Mr. Fairbanks and Mr. Chaplin, who invent their own scenarios and do their own directing, we might seem to approach more nearly the necessary condition. And in the actual process of production itself it may be allowed that there is then, potentially at least, something of the genuine creative excitement. I say potentially, because the basic subject-matter of such productions is nearly always — I should say always, but there may be exceptions of which I do not know — of insufficient vitality to be the occasion of authentically creative effort. Spirit and gusto, of which Mr. Fairbanks's and Mr. Chaplin's work is full, are not, it may be added, the same thing as vitality in this sense. But if a man of Mr. Fairbanks's energy and resource and technical dexterity could be inspired by some really significant conception, it is likely that in production he would, in a necessarily crude but still definite way, achieve the mastery of texture that would afford the true satisfaction to the spectator. To do this on the 'lot' in production is, however, still as far as ever from doing it on the screen. In the studios it would amount to the same thing in essential terms as any other theatrical production, with rather less hope of artistic unity.[1] But with its transference to the screen we are met by the same difficulties that have already been explored. To fall back again on personal experience, I have never in watching a moving picture had any sense of a texture being mastered by an artist, or of there being any texture to master.

I need not apologise for this digression from my

[1] I am painfully aware, as I suppose every writer on such matters must be, of the danger of such words as 'artistic.' But their common abuse does not destroy their proper meaning. 'Artistic,' as it is used in this essay, means pertaining to the imaginative expression of vision, which is art.

theme of the theatre proper. The cinema is a subnect of general discussion in these days whenever the theatre is mentioned, and an analysis of its nature should help us to understand more clearly the nature of the art that we are sometimes told it is to supersede. That it is already a powerful and even critically dangerous competitor of the theatre as a provider of popular entertainment is evident, though the success of such plays as 'The Ringer,' 'The Ghost Train,' and 'Interference' shows that the gentleman in the theatre's corner has a good many vigorous rounds left in him yet, and may get the verdict on points after all even if he cannot hope to win by a knockout. As for the theatre of the imagination, it is for reasons that I have attempted to define in no more danger from the cinema than it is from the Motor Show or the Cup Final.

We can now summarise the outlook with which the playgoer may be supposed to approach the theatre of our time, assuming him to treat it as the home of an art to be respected. So far as the acting is concerned, he will not, by confusing the player with the part, suppose that a small and simple part effectively played deserves more credit than a big and complex one played with here and there a touch of uncertainty. He will admire the actor who can invest a part of no intrinsic value with some interest, but he will admire the same actor more in a part that demands all the wit and imagination that he possesses, and then leaves possibilities unexhausted. He will know that to see the same actor in a pinchbeck part and in a fine one is not to see two aspects of the same talent, but to see two talents profoundly differing in aim and order. The contrast is as great as though the same Stradivarius or Amati should be played on by Mischa Elman and by the second fiddle in a restaurant. And, finally, he will realise that the distinction between good and indifferent acting is largely a matter of detail and variety. Many actors, who have learnt the elements of their craft well enough, never get beyond that because they have not a sensitive gift of invention that can sustain them and the interest of the audience through a long evening's work. They mostly become sound small-part actors, and as such sometimes score notable successes. Occasionally a player with this limitation makes a reputation as a big-part actor by reason of some attractiveness in appearance, voice, intellectual distinction, or personality. There are people to-day high up in their profession who have done this. But what usually happens when such a player is called upon to carry the principal burden of a play is that he has used up all his equipment in the first quarter of an hour and is left *in vacuo* for the rest of the show. The genuinely fine actor is the one who can keep you at the top of your attention through four acts and still be a revelation in the fifth. This implies immense staying power, both in body and mind. Shakespeare recognised this in his well-known practice of resting his big parts for a considerable interval before calling upon them for their supreme effort.[1]

In the matter of plays our playgoer will keep a clear distinction in his mind between those that belong to the theatre of the imagination and those that don't, between those that he goes to see in-

[1] For example, Hamlet, Lear, Othello, and Macbeth, each of whom is off the stage for something like four hundred lines before the final scene of his catastrophe.

stead of reading Hardy or listening to Mozart or turning over his collection of drawings, and those that he goes to see instead of filling up his income-tax forms or playing billiards. He will, further, refer his judgments to a reasonably comprehensive knowledge of the dramatic achievements of the past, and not be too easy in his satisfactions. Since he genuinely enjoys the theatre and is never really bored or unhappy there, he may be grateful for the entertainment even when it is but a middling affair, remembering that the mistakes and shortcomings of the theatre are apparent to the veriest numskull, while a stage production of any sort tells of endless difficulties and patience, and in almost every case of some talent that is worthy of respect. But good-natured tolerance of this kind will not make him the less scrupulous in deciding as to the positive merit of the plays that he sees. He will not apply superlatives of praise to the brilliant all-round efficiency of 'The Ringer' and speak disparagingly of 'The Faithful' because it sometimes stumbles in its great aim. He knows that it is bad criticism to say that 'Mr. Wu,' leaving financial profits out of the question, was a successful play and 'The Sister's Tragedy' a failure, because, although 'Mr. Wu' was more efficient at its own job than 'The Sister's Tragedy,' it is impossible to use the same terms in speaking of the two things. It is like saying that the borough surveyor is a more successful explorer than Columbus. Our playgoer, in short, has standards, and he keeps his mind, however independently, always in contact with them. And now let us go with him to the theatre.

'THE RINGER'

WE will go twice, once to a play of the one sort, and once to a play of the other. And, since I have used 'The Ringer' so frequently by way of illustration, it may as well be our first choice. To start at the beginning, we will book our seats. Twelve-and-sixpence a piece for stalls is rather stiff — we could each buy a substantial new book for that, or even two, or go to the cinema luxuriously four times, or get a new hat. However, this is a night out, so we will do it lavishly, and take our stalls. They are rather far back, in the middle of a row, good for seeing, but subject to inconveniences, as we shall find. The night comes, and we arrive at the theatre. Cloak-room? We think not — it is easier to get away at the end without. Programme? Yes: sixpence each. I remember theatres where getting your programme for nothing you have an agreeable feeling that you are getting your entire evening's entertainment for nothing; not at all a bad speculation for the management. But it seems the programmes are let to someone, who probably lets them to someone else, and so on, and everyone has to get his stiver of profit, and so we pay sixpence. We get into our seats, and study our sixpenn'orths. Looks exciting — Scotland

Yard, Detective-Inspector, Ex-convicts, a Police Station. I contemplate the curtain and the proscenium arch; what a history of the drama's evolution is written there. I go back to the Elizabethan theatre, the Fortune perhaps, with its tiers of spectators ranged in their sheltered galleries round the courtyard open to the sky, the stage with its little balcony at the back under a lean-to roof, and the broad expanse of apron coming far out among the groundlings, so that the actors will declaim the mighty line toe-to-toe with a spell-bound audience, like the tub-orators in Hyde Park. That must have been an excitement indeed for an imaginative people. I once heard Mr. W. H. Massingham describe the electrifying effect produced on his not easily inflamed mind by the spectacle of Billy Sunday crawling on his stomach to the edge of his platform and launching his revivalist fervours on an astonished congregation as he lay prone with distended neck and rolling eyes. It must have been some such contact as this that the Elizabethan actors established with the playgoers who saw the first productions of plays by Marlowe and Webster and Ben Jonson and Shakespeare. And when the occasion of the contact was dramatic poetry of that splendour, the poet, fresh not merely from 'the vasty fields of France,' but from the boundless firmament of life, might with confidence call upon his hearers to:

> Let us, ciphers to this great accompt,
> On your imaginary forces work.

My fancy leaves the Fortune, its flag flying from the turret, as to-day from Westminster to announce that the business of the house is on hand, and comes forward three hundred years to Mr. Nugent Monck's Maddermarket Theatre at Norwich, where one may still see Shakespeare's plays acted on the stage for which they were constructed, and learn more about his art in three hours than in a cycle of London, W. And then back again to the period between this spacious intimacy and our modern picture-frame method, when they had those charming proscenium doors where the players came in and out like the little old lady and gentleman who tell about the weather. Such doors may still be seen at the Theatre Royal (as I remember) in Bristol and, I am told, in one or two old playhouses elsewhere. And as the orchestra begins the overture, my thought turns to the small theatre in Birmingham where they have both the proscenium doors and an adjustable apron, so that any kind of play can be put into action with the greatest possible flexibility of rhythm. Every theatre ought to be equipped in this way, both for possible revivals of old plays and to afford living dramatists ampler scope in their work. Discipline for the artists is good, but not when it becomes a tyranny; and the tyranny of the picture-frame stage does to-day hamper the playwright's legitimate freedom. Any experiment in construction is made impracticable by the mere matter of bricks and mortar. This is not to say that the picture-frame structure is in itself bad dramatically; far too much fine work has been conditioned by it for that. But it has had a long term of almost undisputed authority, and it may well become a lifeless habit unless it is braced by association with other technical methods. The little theatre movement in Europe and America has paid much attention to this problem, but the experiments on the whole have tended towards mannerism and decorative fancy rather than towards the invigoration of playwriting. A good deal of solemn nonsense is talked about expressionism on the stage, plastic values, orchestral patterns, tone distribution, old Uncle Tom Cobbleigh and all; but if the dramatists were given a 'heaven,' a central stage of two platforms, an apron and two proscenium doors, and the means of using all or any of these in combination at will, they would bring far more expansion to the technique of the theatre than these well-meant but rather precious frivolities. We shall not better our condition by dashing about the world to inspect every new lighting apparatus that is invented. The first and probably the only reform that is wanted in the theatre is one that will provide every playhouse with the requirements that I have indicated.

It is satisfactory to hear that the new Stratford memorial theatre is being planned with these features in mind.

But, they will not be required for 'The Ringer' on which the curtain is now going up. Discovered is Mr. Leslie Banks, facing us square-on close up at the front of the stage, half-seated on a table in a Superintendent's room at Scotland Yard, looking rather sulkily handsome in a little black beard. This is a good beginning, showing at once Sir Gerald du Maurier's deft touch as producer, focussing an important figure of the play, as we feel sure he must be, sharply upon our attention at once. And we know, too, what an accomplished and interesting actor Mr. Banks is. A capital and promising start.

The first question is, what is he going to act? Within three minutes of the curtain's rise the answer is sufficiently clear. He is going to act a detective; that is to say, he is not going to act a man of character who happens to be engaged in detecting, but a Simon Pure Detective with a capital D, with no existence beyond the terms of that specification. Almost at once we know that any breath of life that is given to the part will be an incidental contribution made by Mr. Banks himself. We have the measure of the play. It is not to be about people, but about Detectives and, presumably, Criminals, and a Hero and his Donah.

The imagination is given leave of absence, and we settle down in anticipation of a good yarn. Which is very pleasing and, for myself, the best of luck in the circumstances, for to me a good yarn is the most agreeable form of easy entertainment. I would as soon think of missing a new Sherlock Holmes story as of saying No to a Wimbledon invitation. And what with Mr. Edgar Wallace's story, and Sir Gerald du Maurier's eye for a stage situation, and Mr. Banks already with us and Mr. Faber and Mr. Dyall to come, and the general fun of being in the theatre anyway, the occasion is even more hopeful than the later exploits at any rate of Mr. Holmes. That is how we feel at the end of the first three minutes or so. And there is no loitering; another three minutes and the mystery that surrounds 'The Ringer' has us firmly in its hold. We would not miss a moment of it.

At this point a diversion occurs. We are, you may remember, in the middle of a row. The play is one of the successes of the town, and yet just beyond us are five vacant seats. But, happy management, it seems that they have been booked all the time, and their holders now walk over us to take possession. Some of them are stout, so we have to rise and tip up our own seats while they pass. Perhaps it would have been better to leave my coat and hat in the cloakroom after all. For the best part of a minute, that seems like ten, the attention of some twenty-five people, including our own, is entirely distracted from the stage, and by the time order is restored we have effectively been put out of touch with the action. We have probably missed some vital clue. No; the expert producer has reckoned with this contingency, and by arranging that everything in the exposition is said twice sees to it that we shall not be penalised if we through no fault of our own miss it the first time. We are grateful for his consideration.

If anyone thinks that I am now going to summarise the plot of 'The Ringer,' he is mistaken. In the first place, I don't remember it, and, secondly, there is no convention of dramatic criticism so tiresome as that by which intelligent writers are made, surely against their will, to pretend that they can say in a quarter of a column what the dramatist has said in sixty pages or so. It may be laid down as an axiom that no summary of a plot ever has the remotest resemblance to the plot that it summarises. Once we get beyond the small change of conversation there are never two ways of saying a thing that is worth saying at all. In my schooldays there was a dreadful practice of making unhappy small boys translate great poetry into bad prose with a view to educating them.

But while I shall have forgotten the plot of 'The Ringer' three months hence, I do now (which is three months ago) find it very exciting in the theatre. I know that somewhere about the premises, probably among the people who have by now appeared on the stage, is the Super Bad Man known to the police of all the continents by the name that gives the play its title. He is a Robin Hood sort of fellow, it seems, defying every law, but a terror to skunks. It is strongly insinuated by everyone, including the author, that this person is none other than Mr. Banks himself, the Detective. But that very engaging old Scotch doctor is, I observe from the programme, being played, with masterly deception, by Mr. Faber, and I cannot help thinking that it will turn out that the best part, who must be the Ringer about whom they say such dazzling things, has been given to him after all. It is true that a lady who is probably the Donah has also appeared, and although she is the Ringer's young and beautiful wife she takes no notice whatever of Mr. Faber, while she is plainly disconcerted on seeing Mr. Banks, but that is probably only to make it more difficult. To date, my money is on Mr. Faber.

And now, about half way through the first act, a lady and gentleman come in to the two remaining empty stalls. This time the convulsion takes place in the second row, and the newcomers, who it is to be feared must be overworked, have the felicity of disturbing not only the entire house but the actors as well. They sit down, but the gentleman at once rises again to take off his coat, while the lady opens a large box of chocolates which appear to be wrapped up in the best quality parchment. Somebody says Ssh! and there is quiet while we again collect our scattered wits to the action which is now developing at a great pace.

Perhaps, after all, Mr. Faber isn't really the Ringer, but is here for the purpose of catching the Ringer out. But we should only want such a nice old gentleman to catch someone out who was genuinely a scamp, and if the Ringer is that, where are we? For here is Mr. Dyall, so bland and plausible in his amiability, a villain-designate if ever there was one. And that would mean two leading villains in the piece, which would never do. Or stay — is Mr. Dyall the Ringer? Hardly, I think, because then there would be no reason for Mr. Faber to be anything but the venerable figure that he seems to be, and so we should have no proper Hero, and the Donah would have no suitable partner at the end of the play. My money remains where it was, and I grow in the conviction that the Ringer and the Hero are one.

All this speculation is very good sport, but it is becoming increasingly difficult. For a voluble person two rows behind us, who thinks Leslie — she doesn't say which one — is a darling, and hates to see him got up like that, has been to the play before, and has now brought a friend. That is how the success of a play is made, and it is how the reason of less fortunately situated playgoers is threatened. I have already turned round and stared severely at her twice, without effect. She keeps steadfastly five lines ahead of the dialogue, and now, in desperation, I say 'Be quiet, please.' A nervous little banker on my left—I deduce that he is a banker because he wears gold-rimmed spectacles, and I feel no end of a Detective at present, though I have rarely found that it was the banker who was nervous, and my own doesn't wear spectacles at all—starts, and lets me know silently that it would be well for me to practise what I preach. But I don't care, since the chorus behind having dwindled into a whisper which though I can hear it conveys nothing to me, I can enjoy my speculation again.

One thing I note with peculiar interest. Mr. Banks continues to be the Detective at one hundred per cent, and a very polished performance it is. I never know whether the official view that the detectives of fiction are not in the least like the real thing is due to anything but prejudice, but I do know that Mr. Banks is just what I want my detectives to be. He is inscrutable without for a moment being dull, or if not quite inscrutable then only with a pleasing concession to my own agile penetration. He thinks I don't know what he is thinking, but I do; and that is a decided score for him as an actor. He is far too good a craftsman to attract attention to himself when it should be elsewhere, but when it turns to him at some unexpected word or movement he has the gift of making you feel that it comes out of an action from which he has never been detached; you know that he is there even when you are not noticing him. Also his timing is perfect; he is never out of beat with the other players, which of a good actor is not the same thing as saying that they would never be out of beat with him if he would let them. Altogether, one feels, he will impress some critic as the best young man on the English stage, an impression, however, that he will have been by no means the first to make within the past twelve months. But, with all his ability, he remains mere Detective. He makes no attempt to bring his admirably presented automaton to life. Far from blaming him for this, it speaks well for his discretion that he is fixed on attending strictly to business. To confuse the organic with the mechanical is exceedingly dangerous. I intend no offence whatever in using the word mechanical, which best serves the purpose of differentiating the plays that are not concerned with life from those that are. It is not disrespectful to say of 'The Ringer' that it has no organic existence in the way that 'Hedda Gabler' or 'Juno and the Paycock' have. It makes no such claim, and bases its appeal very successfully, as we are at this moment learning, on other considerations altogether. There is a certain elementary cunning in all of us, a survival perhaps of the days when we were at once both hunters and the hunted, that delights in getting the better of opposition. We like to succeed in business, to win games, to be top of the list, not only for material gain, but with ancestral memories of the days when if we did not get a down on the other fellow he would get a down on us. The instinct remains, though it is said to have become more civilised: at any rate we no longer cut notches on our clubs as casually as once we did; but we inherit the zest for outwitting our rivals, and gratify it in business competition, in sport, in solving cross-word puzzles, and in attending such plays as 'The Ringer.' If we see an organic play, our experience is enriched. But Mr. Edgar Wallace does not care a rap about enriching our experience. It is a case of his wits against ours, and what we demand of him is that he shall give us a really good run for our money. This he is now decidedly doing. The intrusion of psychological verities might set us off dangerously in other directions, and they are excluded. Mr. Banks properly conspires in keeping us to the point. His part has its precise place in the contest that is engaging us. He is easily master of all the devices that help it to take that place with complete assurance, and any attempt to do more with it might break up the meeting in disorder. It would never do for the parts of a machine to become animated with ideas of their own.

But, oddly enough, Mr. Faber is doing this. He has wider opportunity for characterisation than Mr. Banks, but there is more in it than that. His Scotch doctor contributes as exactly as the rest of the *dramatis personæ* to the development of the play and our sense of excitement in the plot, but we notice that he is doing something else as well. He is not only a Scotch Doctor, he is becoming a live person who is, or is pretending to be, a Scotchman who has taken up medicine. When Mr. Banks's Detective or Mr. Dyall's Crook go off the stage they go out of existence, on which score we have no complaint against them. When Mr. Faber's Doctor goes off the stage, however, we are vaguely aware that he may be going home, or for a walk in the Park, or to buy some gramaphone records. The others sprang fully armed from Mr. Wallace's head at eight-thirty and eight-forty-five this evening respectively, but this old Doctor was a little boy once and went to school, and grew up, and was perhaps disappointed in love, and has travelled about the world, and probably reads Burns and Charles Lamb. When the Detective says he has been in America we register the fact as a possible clue to our problem, but it has no significance beyond that. When the Doctor says he has been to India, we wonder for a moment what parts of India, how the Rajahs treated him, whether he brought back any interesting souvenirs. If the Detective coughs we take no notice of it; if the Doctor coughs we hope he is taking proper care of himself. Since there are no meals on the stage, there is no reason to suppose that anyone else in the play has ever tasted food, but I find myself unaccountably surmising that Dr. Lomond preferred Ribstone Pippins to Worcester Permains for dessert.

Why Mr. Faber is behaving in this unexpected manner it is difficult to say. Being not only a very good actor but a very experienced one, and having a naturally curious mind into the bargain, it is probable that he finds any temptation to stick a bud of truth on this bush of make-believe irresistible. Whatever the reason why, it is amusing, and instructive, to watch how he does it. When he walks on to the stage, we feel that he has been walking like that for quite a long way, which means that, mentally, he has been doing so. And his attention, though quite loyal to the business of the play, seems not to be exclusively concentrated on it; it is as though he had somehow left part of himself behind him. He opens his mouth as if to form a word, and no word comes; but we are intent because we can see — yes, see it, in his poise or by the way he strokes that far side of his drooping moustache — that the brain is sorting out the words from which the right one will come yet. If he rolls a cigarette, he does not trouble to push back the shirt cuffs that dribble beyond their proper limits and lap over his palms. How uncomfortable that must be. But as he does nothing about it, clearly it cannot be uncomfortable to him; which means that he wears his cuffs like that when he goes for his walk in Hyde Park, when he goes to India, in fact, always. As he is talking his hand goes irrelevantly to his pocket, as though he might be looking for something that he put there the day before yesterday. And by such dots and dashes the code is made up by which communication is established between the Doctor in the play and the Doctor outside it.

But while all this is a striking testimony to Mr. Faber's rare talent, and to the liveliness of his mind, it has a curious effect upon the play and upon us. For we are by now convinced that Dr. Lomond is the Ringer in disguise, and yet Mr. Faber is no longer playing anybody disguised as an old Scotch Doctor, but giving a most convincing performance of an old Scotch Doctor in being. Just a half-glance once and again, perhaps, if you are quick enough to catch it, but no more than that to suggest that he may not be what he seems. Our conclusions are being drawn from the action of the play, unaided by Mr. Faber. If it were otherwise, the play would lose its interest we know, but what is happening is that — if our guess is right — the Ringer is adding to his other accomplishments that of being an exceedingly fine actor. The truth is that Mr. Faber is greatly increasing our enjoyment by giving us a piece of characterisation that is quite apart from the scheme of the play, but that in doing it he is in two respects endangering the slickness of the machine. In the first place he keeps on making us wish we could see him play all sorts of parts that have nothing to do with 'The Ringer,' and then he introduces this anomaly about the Ringer's histrionic abilities. To this extent, he may be said to be serving the play less faithfully than Mr. Dyall and Mr. Banks, grotesque as it may seem to complain of a performance so masterly. And of course we are not complaining at all. To say that he is too good for the play would be unjust to the play's merits and to his own very strict sense of obligation. And yet, in a sense, that is what it comes to. It is for this reason that 'The Ghost Train' leaves a more compact impression on the mind than 'The Ringer.' In the one case we remember a play of a certain attractive type, performed by everyone with an exact appreciation of its necessities; in the other we remember a play of the same type similarly acted, and with it a single performance that did everything necessary with unfailing certainty, but also had qualities that somehow did not belong to the occasion, qualities that kept on calling back the imagination that we had sent off for the evening.

It is, however, not yet a matter of remembrance at all. It is, in fact, the third interval. We go out to stretch our legs, and to buy a light refreshment. Everybody is liking the play very much. Jolly good, is the almost unanimous judgment. One elderly enthusiast thinks that 'The Ticket of Leave Man' was better, and a young lady smoking a cigarette in a long imitation jade holder thinks that Mr. Godfrey Tearle is better looking than Mr. Faber, though she admits that looks don't much matter in this case. A rather florid man, who is, perhaps, a real detective, complains that Mr. Banks takes too much for granted, or more precisely expects us to take too much for granted about him, but then, as has been suggested, detectives, like journalists, always complain that they are misrepresented when they are put on the stage, a view no doubt to be attributed to their well-known kindness to other people. A languid youth with side-whiskers thinks they do this sort of thing better in Paris, but his companion, we are glad to hear, maintains that British goods are best, while a bright looking school-boy of sixteen or so announces that Edgar Wallace is the finest living novelist, but not so good at plays as Mr. Lonsdale, because he thinks Miss Gladys Cooper stunning. Opinion as to the identity of the Ringer is fairly evenly divided between Mr. Faber and Mr. Banks, with a shade of odds on the former, though Mr. Dyall has his supporters, and there is a little miscellaneous punting on obvious outsiders.

Returning to our seats, we are asked very politely to buy an ice-cream or a copy of Mr. Wallace's novel. Having recently spent six months in the U.S.A. and already possessing all Mr. Wallace's novels, I need neither, and turn over the pages of my programme again. It is not one of those frisky magazine affairs that publish Mr. Seymour Hicks serially, but elsewhere display a less consoling wit, nor does it in the manner of the Rean Dean management enrich our intimacy with the ladies and gentlemen of the cast. But it has attractions of its own. I don't find the new dramatic lists advertised, or the Flemish Exhibition at Burlington House, or Mr. Paderewski's forthcoming recital, or any solemnities of that kind. Dental paste, face creams, lingerie and shampoo powders share my attention with the benefactor who will lend me fifty pounds and upwards with no security. Also I ascertain where I can learn to Speak with Confidence, have my eyebrow contours refined, or get Titled Ladies' Gowns. An unusual feature of the programme proper is to be noted: the author's name is in the same type as those of the players and the producer, and only one size smaller than that of Mr. Frank Curzon himself.

The curtain is up on the last act, and immediately the stalls are a hive of industry as the occupants stumble back to their places in the dark from the bars and lounges. A gentleman standing on my toes explains that he has come into the wrong row, and pauses as though for an answer. A suitable one does not occur to me. In a few moments the dance of the fireflies dies away, and Mr. Dyall is evidently making rapid progress on his journey to the dogs. The interest is being very skilfully maintained, and nothing is neglected that can spice it. I like particularly that mysterious red light that keeps on appearing and disappearing above the door, the more so as I am quite unable to discover what it means. But that, I am sure, is because I have been stupid. Mr. Dyall is playing marvellously on a piano, the keyboard of which I cannot see, but when he gets up it is clear that he is shortly going to have convulsions. The red light evidently means a good deal more to him than it does to me. It is now certain that he is not the Ringer, because he is so scared when he is by himself, and whatever the Ringer might pretend in front of other people we know by now that alone he would never give way like this. The action becomes swifter and swifter, and from this point, for me at least, a little confused. But a discreet touch of confusion is always a great help in bringing this kind of play to an end. We must not ask for logic, but for dash and a firm grip that will hustle us over difficulties before we know where we are. Not but what 'The Ringer' may be perfectly logical in its conclusions; I only know that I am losing track of the last movements. Mr. Dyall walks in and out of the wall, and a burglar is breaking in at the window, but it turns out to be Mr. Banks the Detective who has been sent to watch over Mr. Dyall who is the skunk that the Ringer is after. I am sure that there is a good reason why he didn't ring the bell and come in by the front door in the ordinary way, but it escapes me, and in any case it was nice to think he was a burglar. Mr. Faber and what seem to be several policemen arrive, and Mr. Dyall is going madder and madder. I am not sure about the policemen, because they rush on and off, and I can't tell whether they are all one or different. The orchestration of the red light is now extremely good, and something startling must be going to happen. It does; all the lights go out, there is a scuffle and a scream, the lights go up again, and there is Mr. Dyall lying with a knife in his heart and serve him right, and the Ringer with his wig off looking very young and handsome and every inch a Hero, kissing the Donah, and they glide off through the wall, I should have said straight into the arms of a policeman, but there again I must be mistaken. Of course, I can't tell you who the Ringer really was after all.

We agree as we leave the theatre that it has been a highly successful evening. And we decide that next week we will go to 'Juno and the Paycock'; which we do.

'JUNO AND THE PAYCOCK'

It is very soon plain that we are now in an altogether different world. In 'The Ringer,' with the one accidental exception noted, we found that the figures of the play had no life apart from the stage, where they had a very absorbing but mechanical existence. They were used specifically for the purpose of developing an entertaining plot, the plot was not devised for the purpose of showing them as people interesting in themselves. In 'Juno' the characters seem to have got on to the stage by chance, and to have no very clearly defined business there. From the first we realise that they belong to no plot, that, indeed, a plot of any sort is unlikely to be of the smallest use to them. Adopting the same permutations of time as before, I can remember a great deal less about the plot of 'Juno' than I can about that of 'The Ringer,' which is little enough. But, back again now in the theatre, these characters before me, that seem so aimless in their purposes, I am not likely to forget at all. And before proceeding further, there are two aspects of this production that long before the first act is over force themselves on our attention.

One is the speech of the players. In the hey-day of the Abbey Theatre Mr. Yeats used to come sometimes to Birmingham when we were producing his plays, and we talked often of the remarkable impressions that the Irish Players were making not only in Dublin, but even more spectacularly in England and America. And he admitted that their success away from their own environment was due in part to the novelty of their idiom and inflection as they fell on other than Irish ears. Without attaching too much importance to this view, there is unquestionably something in it. The language with which you are familiar spoken in an unfamiliar way and with unexpected turns always has a lively appeal of its own. Every Englishman, for example, thinks that every American has a peculiarly racy way of telling a story, an opinion that is far from being shared by every American. A cockney hearing a native Cornishman or East Anglian saying that it's a dull day and times are bad finds a significance in those commonplaces that would certainly not be there if they were said by one of his own breed. An Irishman can doubtless listen to Miss Allgood and Miss O'Neill and Mr. Sinclair talking on the stage and not be aware that anything unusual is happening in the way of sound, but to the Anglo-Saxon something is happening that is very seductive indeed. The unaccustomed phrasing and modulation, to say nothing of what seems to be a distinctive and lovely quality of voice, give an appearance at least of style to everything that is said irrespective of its meaning. While it is in consequence always delightful to listen to these players, it is often difficult to decide how much of our pleasure is due to the intrinsic merit of the play and its performance, and how much to our own constantly renewed surprise. Whether something of this special satisfaction would wear off in time we cannot tell, though when we see the Irish Players again after a long interval they do seem for a few moments to exercise a spell that is the greater because we had forgotten it. But it takes more than a few minutes, or even a few performances to break it, though it be diminished, and I can personally say no more than that, since it has never been my good fortune to be a regular member of the Abbey audience. I only know, for example, that Mr. Sinclair seems to me not only to be as assured and subtle a comedian as any that I have ever seen on the stage, but that this effect is greatly helped by the fact that if he says 'I must now be going' he does it with a tone and cadence that bring to the announcement a perfection of comic style. It may be, then, that our admiration for these Irish plays is to some extent fortuitous, but with all allowances made the positive merits of such a work as 'Juno and the Paycock' are sufficiently obvious to establish its place in the theatre of the imagination.

THE PRODUCER

THE other question that arises is that of production, and it may profitably be considered with some closeness. Among workers in the theatre there is, perhaps, nothing about which there is so much difference of opinion as the functions of the producer. It is generally allowed that it is essential at rehearsals to have someone whose duty it is to see that the consecutive parts of the action are properly linked up, that the grouping of the figures on the stage is easy and effective to the eye, that the movement and 'business' of each player are so coordinated with the scene in general as not to confuse the interest of the spectator, and that the mechanical devices of the stage manager are strictly in time and place. Even the old actor managers saw the necessity of such supervision, but in most cases they were themselves responsible for their own productions. In plays that had no organic life, and no artistic as distinguished from mechanical unity, this was possible. The chief aim of the production as we have seen was to devise every possible opportunity for the exploitation of the leading actor's histrionic gifts and personality, and it was easy for him to arrange the general movement of the play with this purpose in mind and then to take his place resplendently in the design, as the Koh-i-Nor or the Rose of the Mountains might be displayed by the hand of the setter. In the plays usually affected by the great actor managers, the central or indeed the only interest was directed on the parts that they were to play. The other parts had no independent life; they were there for the sole purpose of contributing to and supporting the effect that the actor manager was to make. Some of these actor managers even went so far as to surround themselves with none but inferior actors, to ensure that no rivalry in talent should detract from their own undisputed hold on the audience's attention. But even when this was not so, the result was the same. People went not to see a play that Irving was acting, but to see Irving act. And afterwards, it was Irving that was remembered, not the play. The 'versions' of Shakespeare as produced by the actor managers show that even if a great dramatist was brought into the theatre he was adroitly manipulated to the governing — or the governor's — intention. Shakespeare in this, as in most things, provides the acid test. It was his practice to dominate a play by a single character, and each subsidiary character is used for the purpose of developing and fulfilling the central character in action. But the life of his plays being organic, the effect of character on character has to be organic also. That is to say, however conspicuous the one character may be and however obscure or slight the other, both must alike have life if the contact is to yield any significance. Osric is a mere scratch on the clay beside the deeply modelled figure of Hamlet, and he is, moreover, invented expressly for the purpose of making Hamlet's presentation yet more complete. And yet Osric has a life of his own, a life by which, and by which alone, he can make his impact on the life of the protagonist, and it is a life that we remember, not nearly so urgently but as decidedly as Hamlet's. When, however, these plays are subjected to the actor manager's pruning, it is precisely this life of the subsidiary characters that is eliminated. That in the process the life of the protagonist is gravely impaired if not eliminated also does not matter from the leading actor's point of view, since there are still left ample opportunities for the exercise of his own histrionic powers, by which, and not by the organic life of a play, he makes his appeal. Looking back some years I can recall two productions of 'Twelfth Night,' one by Sir Herbert Tree and one by Mr. Granville-Barker, and in the one case I remember nothing but a very vivid performance of Malvolio, while of the other I retain an exact impression of a great comedy beautifully balanced and artistically complete.

If, then, the play in hand is one that has no organic life, or, as in the case of Shakespeare manipulated, one in which the organic life has been made negligible, the leading actor can himself do all that is needed in the way of production. If he is skilful as a stage manager, which he almost certainly is, he will do all he can to conceal the essential poverty of his play by elaborate mounting and imposing spectacular devices. He does not need a producer to tell him how best to employ his own gifts in what amounts to a star turn, since he knows this as well as Sir Harry Lauder or Mr. Leslie Henson. And he does not need a producer to keep the life of his character in proper adjustment with the life of the play beyond it, since there is no question of these organic contacts. Let the other people come on and go off at the proper time, be up or down stage as he wants them, know to a moment how quickly or how slowly to take up a cue, heighten or lower the pressure of the dialogue at his bidding, and for the rest keep out of the way and leave the audience to him. To do all this is no easy matter, as every actor who has tried it knows. The method is notoriously successful. For nearly two centuries it controlled the English stage, and to-day there are still players who by its use raise large audiences to regular enthusiasm. But it has no place in the theatre of the imagination.

When, however, the play matters for its own sake, this will not do, and 'Juno and the Paycock' does matter. The producer is Mr. J. B. Fagan, himself a dramatist of distinction, and a manager who for many years has put up a courageous fight for beauty in the theatre. He knows as well as anybody that the actors of an intelligent play need producing no less than the members of an intelligent orchestra need conducting in a Beethoven symphony. And the producer's task is one of subtler apprehension than the conductor's. I do not say that it is technically more difficult. The conductor's musical knowledge implies a more specialised training than the producer's knowledge of the theatre. Sir Landon Ronald, for example, being a man of wits and common sense might conceivably, if he put his mind to it, get some sort of a performance out of the Irish Players in 'Juno.' He probably would not do it very well, but he would not necessarily make a fiasco of it. Mr. Fagan, on the other hand, could conduct the London Symphony Orchestra into nothing but chaos, if indeed he had the slightest idea of how to begin conducting it at all. But, given the technical knowledge, the conductor has to deal with a more formal and consequently less elusive form of expression than the producer. A phrase of music may be played in several ways, though, as I have submitted, only in one right way, and its relation to the general texture of the work may be variously interpreted. In these respects the conductor has as much opportunity as he can want of showing the range and depth of his understanding, but even so his one concern is with what he conceives to be the proper stress and distribution of musical notes, which is a simpler, while, if you like, it is a purer, medium to control than the speech, gesture, movement, the infinite variety of things done on the stage, the hesitances and the silences, the grouping and the timing that together make up the medium that has to be controlled by the producer. A first-rate conductor is willing to give a performance of a classic programme with an efficient orchestra with two or three rehearsals, but no self-respecting producer would undertake to give anything like a competent performance of 'Othello' with an efficient company with less than twenty, and he would probably want thirty. But this is a question rather of complexity than subtlety. The essential difference between the two functions is profounder than this. I am not, let me say, making any claim for one art against another on æsthetic grounds. To talk of music as being a greater art than poetry, or poetry than painting, is scatterbrained. A man may very well be insensible to all the arts but one, and still get all the nourishment that art can afford. I am, with confessed ignorance, using music for comparative purposes at the present moment only in order to try the more clearly to define the producer's problem. Much that I can say may even be used as an argument in favour of music's supremacy as an art, but that does not matter.

Our knowledge of life is founded chiefly on our observation of human society. And it is this knowledge, so gained, that is the material with which it is the principal aim of drama to deal. Personal emotion, operating in a single mind not necessarily with reference to other personalities, commonly finds lyrical expression in literature, and it may be said with some reason that it is the predominating concern of music. The unit of human society is the individual man or woman, the separate entity that functioning by itself achieves lyricism. Philosophically it is, I am aware, a license to speak of a mind as functioning by itself at any time, but clearly in experience there is a distinction between the mood of lonely emotion and the conflict, pleasurable or otherwise, with other minds. It is the dramatist's work to take these units and by showing them in interdependent action to enlarge the significance of each separately, and at the same time to convey to us a cumulative significance resulting from a group of these units in conflict. In other words, the drama may be said to be the fusion of a group of lyrical elements into a richness and diversity of life that none of them can enjoy separately. But each of these elements is a human being for the purposes of the theatre. That is to say, when we see them on the stage we see them as figures of our own daily experience, recognisably like ourselves or our acquaintances. Every member of the audience is, therefore, in the position of being to some extent a specialist in the matter being submitted to his judgment, because human society with the individual as its unit is the one circumstance of which everybody in the world has his own measure of special knowledge. If a composer makes a sound which seems odd to me, I know that it is almost certainly because I know less about music than he does. But if a dramatist makes one of his characters say, to put an extreme case, that he would by choice rather be miserable than happy, the least intelligent member of the audience knows beyond dispute that he is talking nonsense. The dramatist is consequently bound by the necessity of so presenting his argument that it shall be credible to an audience every member of which knows what the general conditions of the argument are. He has the right to demand that the judgment shall not be a hasty one, that if the argument takes an unexpected turn it shall not be dismissed irresponsibly without reflection, but he cannot in the last resort appeal to his own exclusive knowledge against the general ignorance of his audience.

It follows that the dramatist, while he has, in order to interest, to establish contact between his units in a striking or original way, has also to do it without outraging even the most unsophisticated experience. And the great dramatists have always done this. It is true that a new or unfamiliar dramatic technique will sometimes bewilder an audience into denying the truth that it embodies, but that is the accident of a moment. When Ibsen was first presented in England he was hooted, but that was because his constructional idiom was one that was strange to English audiences, not because the life in his plays was obnoxious to the English temper. Shakespeare's technique is in itself a far more elaborate and difficult one than Ibsen's, but since it has been familiar to ten generations of Englishmen any raw English youth or unlettered English adult can understand a Shakespeare play, if it is competently acted, without the smallest difficulty; and he will find, further, that the cosmic vision of life that Shakespeare subdued to dramatic terms is superbly within his own comprehension. Every moment of the play brings him immeasurable enrichment, but it is an enrichment based on his own experience and not on a communicated experience of which he can never know anything but by hearsay.

It is this vivifying contact between the units or characters of a play that the producer has to realise with the utmost nicety or perception, and he, too, has to do it in such a way as to satisfy the critical judgment of an audience that is contemplating a familiar scene. Upon his sense of the precise impact to be made by the characters on each other throughout the play, and his fertility of invention in showing that impact in the clearest and most convincing way, the consummation of the dramatist's purpose depends. It is for him to give air and perspective on the stage to the organic life of the dramatist's creation. He may neglect no touch, however trifling it may seem, that shall combine the parts — the word may be used here in either sense — into a convincing whole. He will meet such special difficulties as that of giving credibility to characters that considered by themselves may sometimes appear incredible. Iago is a classic instance. Unless Iago is adjusted with the keenest insight to the full organic life of 'Othello,' he becomes a monster in whom we cannot be interested. But if he is so adjusted, he is an exposition of character immediately instructive to every man's imagination. The reason why Iago is nearly always played monstrously is that Shakespeare performances are hardly ever subjected to one controlling mind, and Iago is a part that irresistibly tempts most actors to incredible antics if they are left to themselves.

Some actors, I know, object to the discipline of production. They think that they know better than the producer, but they are wrong. I am speaking of good actors and good producers. I am also speaking of good plays. The actor who, because he can act better than the producer, as he generally can, thinks that he knows better than the producer how his acting capacity is best employed in the given circumstances, ought to confine himself to drama where organic life is not in question. The producer must certainly have enough acting intelligence to be able to show what he wants by some example. Nothing is more infuriating to an actor in a difficulty at rehearsal than to be told to do something by somebody who is incapable of demonstrating what he means. You cannot explain an action on the stage, you must do it, but a producer need only be able to do it well enough to put the actor clearly on the right track. A good actor may be able to tell whether he is conforming to the more elementary technical rules, but the best of them cannot be sure, in a play which is organically coherent, that he is taking his proper place in the scheme. And since he takes that place not only by a general understanding of what it is all about, but by an accumulation of calculated effects that are governed by technique, there is no detail or moment of his performance that cannot be helped by intelligent production. It is fair to say that actors usually recognise this, and the better they are the more willing are they in most cases to avail themselves of the producer's coöperation. Most actors know instinctively whether a play has artistic unity or not. If it hasn't, they are apt, with reason, to play each for himself, and in this each is his own best guide if he knows his business. When the star makes his part a solo turn with chorus, the little fellows will do the best they can to snatch a fleeting chance when it offers. There is something pathetic in the anxiety of the small-part actor in such a play when he gets a moment to himself on the stage to make the most of it. But when the actors know that they are all alike contributing not to the exploitation of a single player's talent, but to the realisation of a dramatic conception that they can respect, they are glad of direction that will help to bring them fitly, however inconspicuously, into the design. It is then that they feel how much more exhilarating it is to be using their skill in a fine service than to be trying to make it score by its own unaided virtue, and even the smallest-part actor in such a play is relieved of the discomfort of straining after a possible opportunity, knowing that he is in his moment enforcing an impression of which he can claim to be a vital nerve.

How far, we may now ask ourselves, is Mr. Fagan influencing the production of 'Juno' that is taking place before us? His task is complicated at the outset by a special difficulty. These players have been working together for a good many years now, and they know each other's methods to a shade. This means that in the more superficial matter of technique they give and take with assured precision, and in this respect create an effect of well-regulated efficiency that is itself a delight to watch. But it also means that there is a danger of this effect being used as an end rather than as a means, and here the producer has to be vigilant. Players so accomplished and so experienced, however well-intentioned they may be towards the play, are likely to be impatient of any authority that attempts to interfere with concerted methods that are so directly and so obviously to the taste of an audience. The spectator can no more resist the agile contrast and innuendo of a scene between Mr. Sinclair and Mr. Morgan, than he can the rise and drift of their voices. It is like a perfectly executed passing movement between crack three-quarters. But to the producer, with the organic life of the play steadily in his mind, this very agility may be an embarrassment. And we for our part begin after a time to have a vague misgiving that familiarity with the method might a little impair its effectiveness, as it might that of the Irish speech. It is, though faintly, a reflection upon the production of 'Juno' as an artistic whole that we do afterwards remember performances rather too individually, not indeed as we do those in a mechanical play, but still with a slight misplacing of emphasis. Which suggests that the contacts between the characters have not been completely organic after all, that the art which seems to be uniting them so fluently is a little tinged with an artfulness that conceals imperfect joins.

This is not altogether, or even chiefly Mr. Fagan's fault, and to judge by the satisfaction of the audience, in which I am heartily sharing, not widely recognised as a fault at all. But the consequence is none the less before us. I may here parenthetically remind my readers that I am analysing my feelings as a playgoer at some length with reference to two plays specifically because it seemed desirable to apply the general observations that I have made to particular instances, and these plays seemed to afford as good an opportunity as any that I could recall for doing this. Which is only by the way of apology to Mr. Fagan for putting his admirable work for a moment in question. The consequence of which I speak is that our interest is now divided between the very engaging skill of the Irish Players and Mr. Sean O'Casey's 'Juno and the Paycock,' when there ought to be no division of interest, since the play and the players ought to be indivisibly one. It would be a clumsy exaggeration to say that the players very seriously fail to identify themselves with the play, to become incorporated in it, but they do not succeed completely in doing so. Their sense of the characters that they are impersonating could not be finer, and few dramatists can hope to be so fortunate in the delivery of their lines. In view of these advantages, it may seem no better than carping to suggest that still all is not entirely well. Many people will feel that here is a performance that might reasonably be called perfect, and it would be no great concession to agree with them. And yet every now and again we are aware of a slightly mechanical rhythm where we expect the continuity of growth, and so perfection just eludes us. Mr. Fagan could hardly have helped it, and, as we say, the players would have been more than human if they had wholly refused to indulge a method that seems to register a bull's-eye every time. But when we think of some production that has overcome, or indeed has not been faced with such difficulties, and has no less than here the necessary qualities in players, play and producer, we realise that there is not a sharp but a perceptible difference. Mr. Granville-Barker's production of his own 'Voysey Inheritance' at the Kingsway, for example, had a finishing touch of style about it that was due to the vital dependence of one character on another in the playing. I am not speaking of Mr. Granville-Barker's dramatic construction, nor of the mere technical interplay between the actors, but of the unfailing and essential extension of one personality into another in terms of the action.

THIS reservation apart, both Mr. Fagan and the players seem to have served Mr. O'Casey extremely well. And we soon discover that he is not too easy a dramatist to serve. That he brings fresh credit to the theatre of the imagination is never in doubt. He has considered life and drawn his own conclusions, he has a most diverting instinct for the subtler saliences of character, he has a rich fund of wit, and that sureness of mental and emotional balance that creates humour. A dramatist so fortunately endowed may be relied upon to give us a play quick in its tissues, and when he has further, as Mr. O'Casey has, an easy control of movement and timing, the play will be absorbing on the stage, as 'Juno and the Paycock' is. A living play and stage-worthy — that is cause for gratitude, indeed. The rarest talent in the Irish theatre since Synge, says Mr. James Stephens, and we will allow as much more as Mr. Stephens cares to claim. But with all these merits, a play is none the worse for a clear sense of direction, and this is what 'Juno and the Paycock' lacks. To say that in the larger sense it has no design would be to confuse artistic creation with artistic management. If a man has the genuine impulse from life, if he be truly an artist, his work will inevitably have essential design, even though it be chaotic in its external management. The supreme artists, Shakespeare, Milton, Homer, Dante, and the rest, are able to help our comprehension of their vastest designs by submitting them to a strict and orderly management, which is rather a matter of convenience than a process inseparable from expression. Convenience, that is, both to the poet in his work and to the audience in receiving it. A poet, using the term generically, may be demonstrably great and yet be only fitfully intent on this management. His work may not suffer in organic design in consequence, but it is less easily communicated to other perceptions. It is for this reason that the reader who responds naturally to the sustained flights of great poetry finds that 'Paradise Lost' more readily holds his attention through the long elaboration of the theme than 'The Prelude.' In richness of life Wordsworth's poem is comparable to Milton's, and if its creative design is less masterly it nevertheless asserts itself as the work of one of the greatest constructive minds in English poetry. But in external management Wordsworth's poem is far less deft than Milton's, and its impression as a whole less compact and lucid.[1] It may be said without levity

[1] The fact that 'The Prelude' was only part of a greater scheme that was not carried out makes no difference. It is on a scale large enough to let us see what Wordsworth's method was.

that Milton excelled Wordsworth in showmanship. And showmanship is a quality that even the greatest artists have been wisely willing to cultivate. It need hardly be added that many people bring it to a high state of efficiency without being artists at all.

'Juno and the Paycock,' then, seems to me to be defective in this management. The life that it contains is fertile and interesting, and Mr. O'Casey presents it with a rich variety of pungent detail, but he does not always present it homogeneously. And unity of effect is imperative in the theatre of all places. Mechanical construction is rightly discarded by every dramatist who respects his work, but the playwrights who made it their chief aim realised one necessity at least of the theatre if they neglected all the others. In discarding it the responsible dramatist cannot afford to forget the function that it performed, and he has to devise other means of securing the same result. His most satisfactory way of doing this, and I do not know that there is any other, is by keeping his sense of direction steadily active through all the phases of his play. The superficial confusion that will inevitably result if he fails to do this may not denote a confusion of essential design, but it will almost certainly make that design, more obscure to the audience than it ought to be.

TRAGEDY AND COMEDY

THE confusion in 'Juno and the Paycock' arises, I think, from the fact that Mr. O'Casey has attempted a manner for which there are classic examples, but of which he has not fully grasped the conditions. The intermingling of comedy and tragedy was a practice wholly repudiated by the Greeks, to whom, indeed, it was not considered as an artistic possibility. The Greek instinct in these matters was a singularly pure one, and their practice in this respect is no less suggestive in that they were hardly familiar with the idea of comedy as it is known to the modern world. The satire of Aristophanes is so far removed from the comedy of Shakespeare as almost to belong to a different intellectual category, and yet it is sufficiently distinct from Greek tragedy to make the fact that the dramatists never attempted to fuse the two, a clear indication that they viewed any such purpose as forbidden. The inhibition is the more striking in that from what we know of Greek satire it is nearer in spirit to their tragedy than, say, Shakespeare's comedy is to his tragedy, and so might have been the more readily incorporated in a tragic design.

The dramatists of the modern world, under the commanding example of Shakespeare, have with a few exceptions, Ben Jonson for instance, departed from the Greek rule, and they are justified in their works. I must here try to define as briefly as possible the elements of tragedy and comedy as conceived by the Greek and the modern mind respectively. Tragedy with the Greeks showed the operation of natural law upon mankind, and the catastrophe was consequent upon man's disobedience to the law. Since all men alike were subject to this condition of life, it was not necessary closely to individualise the figures of the drama, and character as we moderns term it was virtually unknown to Greek tragedy. The character which the Greeks said was fate had nothing to do with the personality that is the foundation of character in the modern sense, but denoted the disposition of man towards natural law as interpreted by the Greek mind. The theatre of Aristophanes in the same way knew little of the character that interested Shakespeare. There, too, natural law was the agent by which the figures of the drama were tested, but it was now a natural law particularised in terms of social custom and government, and the conflict was no longer solved by disaster, but by derision. In the satire of Aristophanes man was not a struggling soul visited by the just wrath of the gods and redeemed at last of its errors by compassion excited by the catastrophe, but a buffoon tormented by other buffoons to whom he had been so stupid as to give authority. Thus in both tragedy and comedy the Greek preoccupation was with ideas and their application to society and not with character, or, to gloss the term, with characteristic distinctions.

In the modern theatre, which by Shakespeare's time is in its maturity, the intention of tragedy remains unchanged, but not so the method by which it is presented. The conflict of man with natural law is still the theme, but the tragic hero has become more particularised, more invested, that is to say, with character. The artistic gain or loss is not now in question; we are observing the modification in method. And this particularisation, this character, has acquired an interest of its own. If we take the Jason of Euripides and the Œdipus of Sophocles, we find that in both the conflict with destiny, or whatever we like to call it, is the centre of tragic interest, and that this interest is varied by the difference in story and poetic idiom. But if we take Hamlet and Macbeth we find the central interest at once common to both them and the Greeks, we find difference in story and even, though they have the same creator, in idiom, and we find a further and new interest in each of them as clearly characterised individuals. As I say, it is by no means certain that the modern mind is superior to the Greek by this evidence, but it can hardly be disputed that the distinction between Hamlet and Macbeth as persons is far more definite than that between Jason and Œdipus. And it is this sense of contrast that has become the very substance of comedy in Shakespeare's practice. In comedy the idea still has its place, the governing condition or conditions of life by which the figures are to be tested, but the dramatist's aim is not now chiefly to ridicule the stupidity with which the test is conducted on all sides, but to observe humourously the different ways in which different people will behave under it. So that it may be said, with as much truth as so wide a generalisation can hope to have, that in the modern theatre tragedy is concerned with ideas, comedy with character.

But we have seen that something of this character has been introduced into the tragic heroes themselves. It is, I think, a mistake to suppose that the chief interest of Macbeth is his character and not his tragic significance, but his character, whether it heightens the significance or not, does undoubtedly engage our interest in a way not attempted by the Greeks. Shakespeare used this added interest deliberately as an appeal to his audience, and it is reasonably clear that his view of it was that it was a good thing by this interest to lighten the tragic strain at intervals. And so he went beyond the device of investing his tragic heroes with character, and introduced purely comic figures into his tragedy, and so originated [1] what is known to the melodrama of our own day as comic relief.

It is, however, extremely important to note that while Shakespeare will thus freely lighten or accent his tragedy with comedy, he never for a moment allows us to be in doubt as to whether his intention is fundamentally tragic or comic. The porters and gravediggers, the Osrics and Nurses and Peters may divert us as much as they will, but they cannot confuse our minds as to what the issue before us really is. Ford in 'The Merry Wives of Windsor,' conversely, has all the requisites of a tragic figure, but we are never apprehensive that Shakespeare will allow him to become a tragic figure indeed. It is sometimes suggested that in Malvolio and Shylock there are signs of this divided purpose in Shakespeare's art, but my own conviction is that the actor who makes either of them a tragic figure is misrepresenting the dramatist. Malvolio's arrogance is never more than a matter for laughter, and its correction should bring no sense of catastrophe with it; we should merely be glad to see that a stupid fellow has been brought to his senses, or very shortly will be. We may feel that he is something over-roughly used by the toss-pots, but we should come no nearer distress than that. In the

[1] Not he precisely, but the phase of dramatic evolution of which he is representative.

same way Shylock belongs explicitly to comedy, though perhaps more astringently. His revengefulness ought never to be presented as the passion of a tragic hero, but as the mean cowardly little distemper that it is, and far from being disturbed by his misfortune we ought to feel that he has come very luckily out of a discreditable business. The tragic Malvolio and Shylock are the inventions of star actors who cannot bear to see good parts going begging, and equally cannot bear to appear in what they call an unsympathetic light to an audience.[1]

To return to 'Juno and the Paycock,' the play has by this time got well on its way, and it is apparently a comedy. A comedy, indeed, from which all sentimentality has been excluded, and one that is making a shrewd and often even harsh discovery of character. Mr. O'Casey is keeping his threads admirably together, and if he seems to have left one lying loose we may be sure that he will presently pick it up again with an exact purpose. His comic method is at once generous and precise. The people that he places before us are so very Irish, so minutely specified, and yet our interest in them is so far from being casual or detached. We English folk, we feel, could not behave like that, but we

[1] This is not to deny that in Shylock, at any rate, Shakespeare was making tentative approaches to the great tragedies that were soon to follow.

could so easily be that and behave differently. Here is a dramatist, we assure ourselves, of nothing less than genius. And then he becomes unsteady. What is this that is happening to the comic design? Is this our dramatist of genius, or a reporter of a sensational turn of mind who has escaped from the Irish Rebellion with his pockets full of copy? I hope I need not say that I could not speak or think lightly of the black days of that terrible Easter, nor have I the slightest doubt of the depth of Mr. O'Casey's emotion in contemplating them. But these are not the questions before us. We are watching a play, a play of remarkable qualities, and suddenly something is happening in it that looks like blowing it sky-high. Mr. O'Casey is doubly in danger. In the first place, it is immediately apparent as this smother of shootings and corpses and seductions and funerals surges into the play that Mr. O'Casey's gift for tragic writing is at present in no way comparable to his gift for comic writing. This, indeed, is not tragic writing at all, but the best twopence coloured style of journalism. Like everyone else, I am susceptible to that style; a sensational placard in the street — if it be really in the best twopence coloured style and not some such trepidity as 'Death of a Peer's Daughter' — will catch my penny as soon as anyone's, but I am not going to be put off by this sort of thing by a dramatist who has been setting my imagination all agog.

Mr. O'Casey's comedy is a vision of life translated by an exceedingly witty and aristocratic art; what he mistakes for his tragedy is a fearful convulsion of life vividly reported, but in crude and literal terms. But beyond this, even were the horror of Conolly and his men as beautifully created into tragedy as the charming infelicities of Boyle and Toxer are into comedy, the encroachment of tragedy on this scale would confuse our perceptions. And while we are eager to have our perceptions stimulated, held in suspense, hard pressed and even troubled, we are not willing to have them confused. You may salt your tragedy with comedy, or you may deepen your comedy with undercurrents of tragic suggestion, but you cannot write a play that is both a tragedy and a comedy. Can Mr. O'Casey tell us which 'Juno and the Paycock' is intended to be?

It is this uncertainty that makes him no easy dramatist for the actors and producer to put on the stage. Mr. O'Casey will, I know, not think that anything I have written is unappreciative of a gift that has afforded me with so many playgoers a rare excitement in the theatre. But, to resume our fiction of present attendance at his play for the last time, I cannot help feeling some sympathy with Mr. Fagan and his players as I watch this growing evidence of cross-purposes. The end comes, and I cry 'Bravo!' with anyone, but in three months' time one aspect of 'Juno and the Paycock' will have guttered uneasily from my mind, while the humours are an experience that I am never likely to forget.

PRESENTATION

Reflecting afterwards upon our two visits to the theatre, we find in both productions a general expertness that is happily characteristic of a great deal of work in the contemporary theatre. When all has been said for and against the individual talents of the dramatists, the actors and the producers, there remains the finally concerted act of presentation, and in this we can assert, without the necessity of comparisons, that the average accomplishment of the English and American theatre today is on a high level. I mean for example that neither Mr. Wallace nor Mr. O'Casey could reasonably complain that his play had not been adequately presented to the audience. And a strictly adequate presentation is a far more complicated affair than most people suspect.

In any stage performance, no matter how careful may be the coöperation that has gone to make it, there will inevitably be some margin of compromise between the original intention of the dramatist and the finished product in the theatre. A stage performance, whatever its claim to artistic unity may be, is inescapably dependent to a large extent on an immensely complicated organisation that can hardly be called a machine since it is incalculable and capricious in its working. Let us suppose a dramatist to have a working knowledge of the theatre, and then consider the difficulties that lie between his invention and its expression on the stage. First he has to cast the play. If he is fortunate and can afford to engage whatever players he wants he may do well enough in this respect. For reasons already examined, perfect casting may be impossible in the nature of things, since the actor, no matter how loyally he may submit himself to the part, will always and inevitably retain in his performance something of his own personality that remains outside the author's design. These ideal considerations apart, however, and allowing as we have done that they are an essential condition of the theatre as we know and love it, it may be said confidently that there is no play that could not be satisfactorily cast in London to-day if an open choice were given among players now before the public. But even so, the fact remains that between the dramatist's script and the stage performance there is a constant process of modification that has to be reckoned with. Setting aside accidents of personality, an art such as acted drama which is the result of collaboration differs to some extent from the conception of any single collaborator. 'Juno and the Paycock' did not mean precisely to Mr. Fagan what it meant to Mr. O'Casey, it did not mean to the company precisely what it meant to Mr. Fagan, and to no two members of the company did it mean precisely the same thing. The consequent modifications may do a play no harm, it may even do it good, but they are an anxiety to the dramatist and to everyone else concerned. If the original impulse survives them and is finally communicated from the stage to the audience, a feat of considerable intelligence all round has been achieved, and it is a feat by no means uncommon in our theatre. Whether it is more or less so than formerly we cannot tell. Sir Johnston Forbes-Robertson recently said in public that the general standard of acting was unquestionably higher to-day than it had been when he first went on the stage, and one has a feeling, perhaps a groundless one, that in recent years the standard of presentation — that is, of fidelity to the dramatist's intention — has risen also. To secure his fidelity in spite of the difficulties indicates an intelligent devotion to a common cause that can make the theatre the most inspiriting place in the world to work in. For the difficulties are constant, and may easily end in confusion unless there is in everyone an indestructible good faith. Speaking from my own experience, I have been responsible for the production of something over sixty plays. I have been very fortunate in the players with whom I have worked, and I have never found them unwilling to fall in with my views. And yet it is not an exaggeration to say that of all the hundreds of parts in which I have worked with the actors at rehearsals, I have not in a single case, by the time the first performance came, got exactly the result that was my original intention. That it may often have been a better result is beside the point, which is to show the nature of the difficulties peculiar to stage production. When it is further remembered that in every case the author — even when I happened to be the author myself I may add — would no doubt have found me as producer already taking unintentional liberties of my own, the complexity of the problem needs no further emphasis.

There is, too, the question of the scene. The dramatist whose medium is words, when he is creating really thinks very little about his scene at all. In essentials, it may almost be said that one place is as good as another for the operation of his figures and events. As a wide generalisation it may be conjectured that more often than not the dramatist selects some arbitrary scene and proceeds to forget all about it, except for practical purposes which increase in importance as he declines from organic to mechanical construction. A street in Venice, the plains of Troy, an Irish inn, a Mayfair lounge, what you will, these are, or may be, no more than the spin of a coin to the dramatist's imagination. But such shadowy habitations have to become solid and exact on the stage. A new mind is brought into the bargain. All may still be well, but here is yet another hint of necessary compromise. And there are others, supplied by the electrician, the fly-man, the prompter, the wardrobe-mistress, the property-master, the gentleman on the cornet, the heigho the wind and the rain. Thus there is none but a hazardous way for the dramatist in the theatre, and yet he must not be detached or superior about the obstacles. There they are, and to disregard them is to come to grief. The sensible dramatist will familiarise himself with them by actual work in the theatre. Such knowledge, far from resulting in what is called theatricality, is the surest safeguard against it. The dramatist who knows the difficulties of the stage knows also how to take them in his stride without having consciously to invent elaborate means of overcoming them. The theatrical plays are usually written by the dramatists who know nothing about the theatre, or by those actors who know about nothing else. It is our good fortune as playgoers to find that many dramatists do learn the craft of the stage for themselves, and further that the standard of presentation in our theatres is such as to make us suspect the dramatist who complains that his work has been ruined in production. My own opinion is that serious misrepresentation of a play in a reputable theatre is exceedingly rare.

ART AND POPULARITY

The insistence in this essay on the distinction between the theatre of the imagination and the theatre as popular entertainment, the theatre that stands for a great art and the theatre that does not, may renew the old suspicion of art as being something proposed for the satisfaction of the few. If we enjoy the popular theatre without being solicitous for its welfare, if, for example, we view with equanimity the effective competition of the cinema with the theatre of commerce, and yet are jealous for the stability of the smaller theatre that relatively takes hardly a shilling of public money in the pound, does it not appear that we admit our chief concern to be with an activity to which the majority of men are indifferent? Very well; there is no advantage to be gained in denying it. Shelley knew what he was saying when he proclaimed the poet to be the unacknowledged legislator of the world, but Shelley knew as every artist knows that art has never busied itself about the conversion of mankind to its direct influence, or been in the least disconcerted by the fact that while almost everybody is potentially susceptible in some degree to its appeal, it is a small minority in any age that responds to it with eagerness and understanding. To deplore this is to waste our energy on unrealities. There is a point at which consideration of what might be collapses into futile transcendentalism; the really alert and constructive mind prospers in recognising what is. And the evidence of what is in this matter is clear. The most popular form of literature in our time is the novel. At this moment the most popular novelist of artistic importance in this country is probably Mr. Galsworthy. A new book by him reaches a sale here of, say, seventy thousand copies; a lot of these are bought by people who never read to give to friends who don't want them; on the other hand, a large number of them find more than one reader. Three readers a copy is a liberal estimate; which amounts to two hundred thousand in an adult population of I suppose thirty million, or two readers in three hundred people. And even so, one of them is influenced not by natural taste, but by a belief that to read Mr. Galsworthy is the intellectual thing to do. In what is with some reason called a fiction-loving age, it is doubtful whether 'The Forsyte Saga' finds more than one genuinely perceptive reader in five hundred people. When we leave the best-sellers among the serious artists the figures become grotesque. I wonder whether Mr. Ralph Hodgson would sell five thousand copies of a new book of poems, or one for every six thousand of the population, and Mr. Hodgson is one of the best as well as being one of the least difficult poets of the age. Directly the broadcasting programmes include anything above the level of 'The Rosary' the British public debauches itself in a flight of postcards with an orthographic preference for 'eyebrow.'

The theatre has an even more democratic appeal than novel-reading, and yet 'The Farmer's Wife,' which is one of the plays spoken of as drawing all London, in fact during the twelve hundred odd performances of its sensational run drew, I suppose, less than a million people, or one-seventh of all London in over two years. Allowing this most diverting play to belong to the theatre of the imagination, we may reckon that there are usually some five or six such plays to be seen in London, and if they enjoy the same attendance, which is doubtful, we find that the average London citizen goes to the theatre with even the most casual artistic intention about once in three years. If this is how things are in so popular a pursuit as playgoing, how can we pretend that art is ever for the masses? In its more secluded aspects the masses are not even aware of its existence. How many people in England to-day know who William Simmonds is? How many could tell a Henry Ninham from a George Chambers drawing? What income does Paul Nash make? Why does a manuscript page of Mr. Rudyard Kipling's verse fetch two hundred and fifty pounds in the sale room when a page of Sir

William Watson's would probably not fetch more than as many shillings? What is to be said of a public taste that makes Sir James Barrie [1] some part of a millionaire and throws Mr. W. H. Davies on to the Civil List, that turns London streets into pandemonium on the arrival of Tom Mix and lets Charles Doughty be followed by half-a-dozen people to his grave? Great art is for the few, because only the few want it. The supreme solace and inspiration that man has created for his fellows, it is there freely for the delight of as many as will take it, but for the multitudes it means nothing. I do not say that it could not conceivably mean anything, or that the efforts that are constantly being made by earnest folk to widen its influence are wholly misguided. It is true that there are always some people to whom art means nothing because for one reason or another they have never really come into contact with it, and anything that induces such minds to do so is obviously worth while. But the artists themselves, and most of the people who, without being artists, find art a necessity and not merely an agreeable diversion in their lives, are apt to lose interest in proselytising before they are thirty. Mr. Max Beerbohm alone could have invented the spectacle of Mr. Gordon Craig calling Mr. Charles Frohman to repentance.

[1] Need I say that these references to Mr. Kipling and Sir James Barrie are made only for purposes of proportion?

This, however, is far from being a defeatist attitude. Allowing that the artist when engaged in his work should be thinking of nothing else, we must allow also that when he is finished he wants to get about and carry its cause into the world. There is plenty of opportunity for him to do so. Without troubling himself about the millions who do not pay any attention to art, he can occupy all the spare time he wants to in arguing with the thousands who do. And although there are notorious cases of genius being neglected almost to starvation point, and others not yet notorious but likely to become so to our posterity, a great many good artists get along very well without being known to the masses at all. That a first-rate novelist should sell only seventy thousand copies of a book among a population of thirty millions shows conclusively that the great majority of people care nothing for first-rate fiction, but it does not mean that Mr. Galsworthy is worried about his rent or finds time heavy on his hands for want of public notice. Mr. Nigel Playfair's following is not, as these things go, a very large one, but it keeps him fully occupied and brings him as much reputation as he can desire. Mr. John Oxenham sells, I believe, about a hundred thousand copies of a book of verse; Mr. Lascelles Abercrombie's 'Emblems of Love,' published fifteen years ago is, unless I am mistaken, still in its modest first edition, or out of print. Upon which circumstance comment is unnecessary, though it may be observed that Mr. Abercrombie is the first poet whom an English University has had the courage to elect as such to its chair of English literature.

Great art is for the few, but for a few sufficiently numerous and powerful to establish it firmly in the life of the community. This is so in the theatre as elsewhere. A serious dramatist may now and again be lucky enough to score a great popular success, but serious drama does not depend on such occasional prizes. The theatre of the imagination might be far better organised than it is, but even as things are it finds a public that somehow manages to keep it alive. There are to-day in England alone at least a dozen dramatists of proved merit who find it possible to go on writing the plays that they want to write. It is true that they cannot be as sure of getting them produced as they should be, but at least they can hope, taking one chance with another, to keep in business. That they should not be in an even securer position is, indeed, discreditable to the theatre. Mr. Allan Monkhouse, Mr. Granville-Barker, Mr. St. John Ervine, Mr. J. O. Francis, Mr. Halcot Glover, to mention no others, all have plays at this moment that no manager has had the enterprise to produce. St. John Hankin no longer needs encouragement, but what does the present generation of playgoers know of his work, which is as distinguished as anything done in English comedy since Congreve.[1]

[1] One says Congreve as a matter of course, but, since seeing Mr. Playfair's revival of *The Beaux' Stratagem*, one realises what a serious rival Farquhar was to the master of Restoration comedy.

THE PRINTED PLAY

The mention of Hankin leads us to a subject in which every modern playgoer who respects the drama is interested, namely, the printed play. If Hankin cannot be seen in the theatre, at least he can be read, and since literature has come back to the stage the dramatists who have helped in the reconciliation have been publishing their plays whether they get them acted or not. The practice is an old one, and has never fallen wholly into disuse, but it has undergone many vicissitudes. It began in the early days of the theatre. The records of pre-Shakespearean days are slight, and insufficient for any sure generalisation. Printing, in any case, was then a difficult matter, and doubtless the great body of acted plays remained in manuscript. With the coming of the Elizabethans, however, it was the almost universal custom for the poets to print their plays at the time of production, or at least to find them printed with or without their leave. Although the drama of the time was great literature, it is doubtful whether it was then generally recognised as such by cultivated readers, and the printed plays were hardly more than handy books of the words, sold for a few pence and so little cared for by their purchasers that many of them have been lost altogether or become so rare as to be fantastically precious bibliographical treasures. The Restoration dramatists continued the practice, and from their date onwards through nearly two centuries a flood of dramatic rubbish came from the press, brightened only at long intervals by the contributions of a Goldsmith or a Sheridan. It was not until our own time that the dramatists again took to publishing their plays as serious literary productions, and not merely as something to be bound up in the theatre programme. It is, indeed, by no means certain that this has not now become a common practice for the first time.

There may have been exceptions, but it may be taken as a general rule that the Elizabethan and Restoration dramatists while they always published their plays, always did so in immediate conjunction with a theatre performance, usually after rather than before the event, but hardly ever independently of it. The title pages of such printed plays as have survived from those eras commonly refer to the play's production on the stage, in some such terms as this: 'As it is acted at the Theatre in Lincoln's Inn Fields by His Majesty's Servants.' The great Victorian poets, most of whom wrote plays, also published them, but without any hope of, or, indeed, desire for, theatre performance. They were plays written away from the theatre with no reference to its technical conditions, and given dramatic form rather by accident than otherwise. So that the Victorian example makes no matter. And now in these later years the practice has been governed by new conditions. The serious dramatists of the new theatre have all written their plays with the intention of seeing them on the stage, but they have also published them as a separate venture, often before they have gone into the theatre. A generation ago this would have been considered folly, and would have been forbidden by the managers. The superstition that to publish a play before production is fatal to its chances on the stage still prevails in many minds. It originated with a natural assumption that plays which, whatever their acting qualities, were invariably ill written, would be dismissed as worthless if they became known in print before they were seen on the stage. But the plays of the new dramatists have not only brought distinction to the theatre, they have also taken an important place in contemporary literature. With a very few exceptions the acted plays of the eighteenth and nineteenth centuries had no literary merit at all, and in the great ages of the sixteenth and seventeenth it is doubtful whether the printers who supplied the theatres with copies of Shakespeare or Congreve found any public to speak of beyond the audience. But to-day a printed play by a reputable dramatist will readily find a publisher even though it has no immediate prospect of stage production. Mr. Shaw and others have a considerable public that knows nothing of their plays in the theatre, and some of them incorporate an elaborate commentary with the text exclusively for the benefit of readers.

There is a danger, if not imminently, in this state of affairs. The return of literature to the theatre is highly a matter for satisfaction, and it is well that good plays should attract readers as well as playgoers. But if the public demand for the printed play as an independent form should grow, it is possible that dramatists who even in these regenerate days are seldom sure of theatre production may be gradually tempted to a form a little more ample and discursive than is appropriate to the stage, and so drift away again with literature from the theatre. The apprehension probably does not amount to much, but we find ourselves asking questions when a dramatist of Mr. Granville-Barker's experience prints a new play and is apparently indifferent as to what, if anything, happens to it in the theatre.[1]

The publication of plays is attended by another danger less serious but more immediate, and it is a danger that lends some show of reason to mana-

[1] Hardly indifferent; rather, perhaps, of the ominous opinion that there is no place for it in the theatre, or no place that he thinks suitable to its requirements. The play, which has a deep if somewhat discouraging beauty, is *The Secret Life*.

gerial objections. The reading of a play needs a special visualising faculty which cannot be common, and is not constant even in the trained reader. It is easier in the play than in any other form of literature to slip over passages as insignificant that are really of essential importance. This is why many authors strongly dislike having their plays read in the first case even by the most discerning of managers, and prefer to read them aloud themselves, often very badly. The disabilities of some readers is, however, no sufficient reason for discarding a good practice, and most dramatists continue to face the risk of being misread rather than forego the opportunity of being read at all. As I write, a striking instance of how great the risk is comes before me. A critic in 'The Nation,'[1] in reviewing the book of the recently produced play 'Yellow Sands,' by Mr. Eden Phillpots, says: 'How two writers,[2] one of such achievement and the other of such promise, could have collaborated in writing it; how, having written it, they could expect it to amuse anybody; and finally, how their expectations could turn out to be justified; these, in an ascending scale of difficulty, are the problems which face one.... "Yellow Sands" is not only amateurish and sentimental, it is dull. The dialogue is of a banality which, if it were a little less natural one would set

[1] Mr. Edwin Muir.

[2] Miss Adelaide Phillpots is part author.

down to design, and it is made still more unendurable by the poverty of incident in the play.' Mr. Muir is a critic who has paid much attention to the principles that govern literary expression, and it is a form of enquiry that I, with many other people, find very engaging. No artist, and no intelligent reader, can fail to add a zest to his occupation by having lucid theories about the work that he creates or enjoys. But when a man allows æsthetic theory to govern his experience at the cost of common sense, he is apt to become ridiculous. I assume that Mr. Muir has not seen 'Yellow Sands' in performance, otherwise even his disdain could hardly have survived the blandishments of Mr. Hardwick, Mr. Vosper, Miss Richmond, Miss Veness, and the rest. But that a reading only of the play could have produced the impressions on anyone that it has on Mr. Muir is astonishing. A play that has two intricately developed love stories, a strong political conflict, a regular orchestration of domestic feuds, a tea-party, a free fight, the reading of a will in the presence of a ghost, several fits of hysterics and the impact of a substantial legacy on young Bolshevism, could, one would have supposed, scarcely be charged with poverty of incident. If Mr. Muir suggests that the incident, although crowded, is trivial, the answer is that triviality of incident in drama is the consequence of action that has no relation to character, and that in 'Yellow Sands' the network of incident encloses character with remarkable skill. The political argument may at times be superficial and the passions displayed may be unvexed by modern quackery, but nothing happens that is not directly referable to characters that are assembled in a group of genuinely comic invention. And what does Mr. Muir mean by saying that the dialogue is banal? Its style is not notably distinguished, and its aim, in keeping with that of the play as a whole, is never to make psychological discoveries in perfect felicity of phrase. But it succeeds all the time in presenting the homely figures of the comedy with freshness and point. To be prevented from enjoying 'Yellow Sands' by æsthetic principle is to be theory-ridden indeed. To confuse it with comedy that stirs and troubles the depths, with such a play as 'The Playboy of the Western World' for example, would be absurd, but not to be amused by it in the theatre denotes an intellectual aloofness approaching sterility, and if a critic misses this entertainment in the printed book the inference is that he is not a competent reader of plays. Mr. Muir asks: 'How can a performance so dull amuse such a large public.' Which suggests that he has seen the play in the theatre after all, though he may be using the word performance in another sense. However that may be, he favours us with an answer to his own question. 'The faults of the play,' he observes, 'are popular faults. It is written for the man in the street, and might have been written by him. Those who go to see it, one imagines, take it to their hearts. They are not amused; rather they feel at home.' Does Mr. Muir really suppose that it required no gifts beyond those possessed by the man in the street to write 'Yellow Sands'? And what discredit is it to a play that those who go to see it should 'take it to their hearts'? And what justification can there be for saying that an audience, made up of all sorts and conditions of people, that laughs continuously for nearly three hours is not amused? And why do so many people of insight in other respects make ninnies of themselves when they write about the theatre? Mr. Muir speaks of the man in the street, the man, that is to say, of average intelligence, with a condescension that some of his work may entitle him to assume, but in such flowers of nonsense as these he reminds us that there is intelligence below as well as above the average.

THE PLAYGOER AND THE AUDIENCE

ENOUGH now has been said, within the scope of my present design, of the spectacle that the playgoer beholds, and of the mental equipment that he may be expected to have in judging it. But before concluding this essay, we may consider him a little more fully not as an individual, but as a member of the corporate body known as an audience. One of the most sensitive writers now practising as a dramatic critic, Mr. Ashley Dukes,[1] in a recent book on the drama, says of audiences: 'There is no shadow of reason in regarding them as anything but a gathering of individuals with individual

[1] Mr. Dukes has in the last two or three years made a considerable reputation as a dramatist. Ought a man who is writing plays successfully in the theatre to carry on the profession of dramatic critic in the rough and tumble conditions of journalism? I doubt it. Such a book as the one by Mr. Dukes to which I am now referring is a perfectly proper undertaking for the dramatist. But it is another thing to commit himself to a job in which he is often compelled to speak unfavourably of work that is directly in competition with his own, and this without mature consideration. Each man may be supposed to know his own business best, but I am always sorry to see a dramatist of good gifts laying about him when confronted by another dramatist's work, however inferior it may be. To point out what he takes to be defects in a production that in many respects he admires is well enough, but the working critic has often to write without any admiration at all; when, if he be himself a dramatist known to the theatre, most becoming to him would be the silence that his duties will not allow him to keep.

tastes.' But he has previously spoken of 'this visible assemblage of spectators, this momentary unity of tastes, in a word this collective response that distinguishes the drama from other forms of art.' There seems to be some confusion here, and it is no reproach to Mr. Dukes that he is a little uncertain in his mind about an exceedingly obscure problem. Mass-psychology is so elusive in its elements as to be the despair of the subtlest enquiry. We can only make our own scrutiny, drawing from it deductions necessarily indefinite. Where Mr. Dukes and many other writers have failed, or partially failed, I cannot expect to succeed; I can but add a few observations to the general stock.

We playgoers, then, are admittedly separate individuals as we sit in the theatre; we do not wholly lose our identity. The individual may hardly even be conscious that there is anyone else in the theatre besides himself and the players. He may be sincerely convinced that his impressions are not affected by his fellow playgoers, and that his judgment is being exercised in isolation. It is probable that under cross-examination almost every playgoer would admit this to be his view of his own experience. And yet there is definitely an energy at work in the theatre that cannot be accounted for by the fact that a large number of individuals have assembled not only with a common intention of seeing a particular play, but also with a common faculty for preserving their mental and emotional independence. This energy is The Audience, and like Cowper's Jehovah, it moves in a mysterious way; mysterious, indeed, beyond the full understanding of any one of its component minds. My own theory, which I do not advance dogmatically, but after as close an investigation of the subject as I can manage, is that in a gathering of spectators in the theatre two separable activities are at work; the one governed by the emotions, the other by the reason; the one yielding and receptive, the other reserved and sceptical; the one discarding experience, the other testing by it. It was very proper for Hamlet to warn his Player against splitting the ears of the groundlings lest he should grieve the judicious, 'the censure of the which one must o'erweigh a whole theatre of others.' But every dramatist, Shakespeare no less than the author of 'Abie's Irish Rose,' is aware that before the judicious can be brought to grieve or rejoice in the theatre he and the groundlings have to be held together in fixed attention by what is taking place on the stage. And this attention is held by an emotional appeal that is directed not at individuals but at The Audience. This is an essential condition of the theatre, and the fact that it is often exploited to base ends does not exempt the judicious from its operation. It is a condition that has little, if any, reference to the reason, evolving from the crude but inescapable force with which the actor makes his first and most direct contact with the spectators. As we sit in the theatre our attention is engaged by the acting, that is to say the movement, the speech, the actual presence and even the personality of the actor, before we can apply it to the nature of the thing acted. If the acting be skilful, which implies opportunity provided by the dramatist, we, judicious and groundling alike, make this first response before we decide whether our reason is being persuaded or outraged. A play may be rich in qualities and, failing in this respect, be damned; it may be worthless in all else, but succeeding here run for three years. In the one case it may win golden opinions from the judicious outside the theatre, but it fails to please The Audience in it and comes off in a fortnight; in the other it may be covered with intelligent ridicule, but it may make a million pounds, as 'Abie's Irish Rose' is said to have done.

I shall, I hope, not be suspected of confusing my values. My point is that there is, apart from individual spectators, such a thing as The Audience, that it is incorporated into a unit by the most elementary appeal of the theatre, and that its suffrage, often disregarding the opinions of individuals who themselves have nevertheless helped to bestow it, may establish a play to the tune of a million pounds' profit. A million pounds is a good deal, but a play that earns that may very well earn nothing else, and happily the artist would consider the bargain on those terms a bad one. The monetary value of a work of art, as of anything else, is precisely what anyone with the money chooses to give for it. A fool may give forty thousand pounds for an inferior Gainsborough and a man of taste get a fine Cotman for a hundred. No indication whatever is here of the artistic merits of the pictures, but it is idle to say that there is none of their money values, since the fool's money is as hard as any other cash. In the theatre money is made by a great variety of plays but it is never made by a play that does not first of all establish contact with The Audience as an organism distinct from its individual members. Mr. Dukes is right in saying that no one can predict what will and what will not establish this contact, and that the only sane policy for a manager is to back his opinion instead of scuttling about in frantic efforts to discover what the public wants and so addle his head with delusions about 'crowd psychology.' But it is another thing altogether to maintain that this crowd psychology does not exist in the theatre, that an audience is nothing, to quote Mr. Dukes' words again, but a gathering of individuals with individual tastes. It manifestly is something besides that, and the fact that it is so has an immeasurable influence on the nature and the fortunes of the theatre. A manager may be told on all hands that his play is rubbish, and yet console himself against general assurances that no one in the audience likes it by the plain demonstration that The Audience does.

The one judicious has principles and a sense of style, and it is to these that he submits a play when he ceases to be The Audience with the groundlings and becomes himself. This is not the reasoned statement of experience which has been referred to as being the critic's function, but part of the reaction to experience in the theatre. It may be stated, somewhat loosely, that every spectator in the theatre is part of The Audience; that most of them are that and very little else; and that a few are that and also independent arbiters. But The Audience, as such, has neither principles nor a sense of style; it has only an alert susceptibility to the spell of acting. It may be emotionally convinced without the satisfaction of any intellectual standards, without indeed having any such standards. But having them or not, emotionally convinced it must be before they can be applied, and if it lacks them the momentary pleasure of the emotional conviction is not diminished. Let the play be rubbish, there is still a pretence that we are being asked for our opinion, though it be a pretence only. The Audience has an agreeable feeling that it is pronouncing its verdict impartially, not knowing while it is being delivered that its powers of good judgment have been carefully corrupted by the manipulation of the theatre, that in fact it is not expressing an opinion at all, but yielding to blandishments that may or may not be legitimately employed. The unmarried mother is at the crisis of her fate. The hero exclaims that, however touched our human sympathies may be, the fabric of the state must be supported, and that unless a courageous stand is made without sentimentality against these inroads upon morality all safeguards will be destroyed, and society tumble in dishonoured ruin about our ears. We know the hero to be a good man, disinterested and public-minded in his motives, and there is loud applause. Or again, the same mother with the same child is at the same crisis. And the hero heaps his scorn upon a narrow-minded and pharisaical world that in its servitude to conventions and shibboleths will cast out a woman who, in the name of love, has done a perfectly natural thing. And again, there is loud applause. Either situation may be incidental to a great play. On the other hand, either may take place in the theatre without anything of the smallest artistic consequence happening. But, great play or rubbish, effective acting will for the moment insinuate either situation into the emotional conviction of The Audience that as The Audience is serenely indifferent to convictions of any other kind.

While, however, not to recognise this peculiar power residing in The Audience is to neglect a vital constituent in the life of the theatre, it becomes on recognising it all the more necessary to examine the claims of popular judgment. The commercial manager, who wants to get his share of as many million-pound plays as he can, cares not a rap for the judicious or his opinion. Let The Audience break into punctual and nightly applause, and he is profitably content to abide by that decision. He, like his play, may be rubbish, but at least nobody in a competitive world can call him a jackass. So long as he is frank about himself he is rather an attractive fellow; it is only when he apes an interest in art that he becomes offensive. A theatre manager either cares about money most or about drama most. If he cares about money most, he does not care about drama at all. If he cares about drama most he may, if he has some money, make a good deal more, but he will never compromise to save his last two hundred pounds. If fine drama has broken him he may do anything down to laying the odds to keep himself alive, but he will not do it by debauching the theatre. I can imagine Sir Barry Jackson or Mr. Nigel Playfair taking half-crowns at Epsom, but I cannot imagine them taking half-crowns for plays that they knew to be good for nothing else.

The commercial manager's natural attachment to The Audience, however, is no excuse for the flattery that is lavished on that decisive power in the theatre by people who ought to know better. We are all good democrats in these days, but democracy has much to answer for, and nothing more odiously than the deference of instructed to popular opinion. Newspapers that want a million readers, managers that want a million pounds, and politicians that want a million votes, have to indulge this most abject of sycophancies or close down, and so we are accustomed to hearing leader-writers, impresarios who are the public's humble servants, and platform rhetoricians joining in a servile chorus dedicated to the sublime intelligence of the average man. The public — which means those members of the public in the majority, the average men — is daily told that its will is law, which indeed for the demagogue it is. Private feuds are conducted with extreme effrontery in the public name; if one of the adventurers of Fleet Street wants to attack a rival, he begins by announcing that the public patience with the transgressor is exhausted. The domination of the average man in the commercial theatre has even overshot itself in the cinema, and there reduced the intellectual level to that of the morons and the hicks. All but a few politicians think and speak habitually in terms of an election address, which is designed for the express purpose of making every man believe that he is as good as anyone else, as for purposes of voting he is. It is said that in a famous business house every employee is given imperative orders to 'remember that the customer is always right.' This sort of thing can be demoralising enough, but in a democratic society we can see how it comes about and afford not to be too impatient of it. In deciding for democracy our western civilisation has decided that the ordinary business and machinery of life shall be regulated by the people, which puts the average intelligence of the people in power and makes it the object of general flattery. The demagogue, in the very act of persuading the public that it is Cæsar, is exhibiting talents that are exceptional and should make him suspect to the levellers whom he addresses; but the groundlings do not see this, and he can afford to laugh at the judicious one who does see it and sees through it, since to one man is ordained one vote. He is exploiting the mentality to which he so touchingly defers, but after all he is exploiting it, ostensibly at least, for purposes proper to its position in the state. If he is given power, it is definitely as a representative of that mentality, and answerable to it. He may laugh at his dupes, but if he does he has to be careful that it is only up his sleeve. The demagogue is what democracy deserves, and on the whole democracy with the demagogue in its midst is as satisfactory a way of getting the world through its day's business as any that has been yet devised.

When, however, the artist turns demagogue, he destroys himself. In fact the artists do not betray themselves in this way, but they are in constant danger of betrayal by others who affect a genuine interest in the arts, and they are themselves led too often into concessions, not, fortunately, in practice, but in doctrine. In the theatre the average man — the average man in each of us — is The Audience, and as such he largely controls the theatre's commercial destinies. But while he is the index by which we know whether a play has the first indispensable element of success, his judgment is of no value whatever in any other respect. Before it can be that, he has to be no longer merely part of The Audience, but the individual with individual tastes and knowledge of whom Mr. Dukes speaks. This is a progression usually beyond his reach, or even his desire. Left to himself, he is content to turn thumbs up or down with The Audience and go his way. He has recorded his emotional response, and does not want to do more. The trouble is that this record being of such importance to the box-office, people insist on treating him as though he were a competent judge of art, while knowing quite well that if he sees a rubbishy play and a fine one, he is as likely as not, if they both hold his emotional attention, to prefer the bad to the good one, or not to know which is which. The dramatist who begins to ask himself, while he is working, what

The Audience is going to think about his play, forfeits all claim to any other attention. Happily, as I say, the serious dramatists don't do this. They rightly use all the skill they can to make The Audience take notice of what they have to say, but beyond that they will not go; what they do say they decide for themselves. But it has in the later days of the new theatre, become increasingly fashionable to affect an intellectual distrust of the intelligence, to say that after all great art is popular art, to discover unsuspected rhythm in musical comedy and the revues, in short, to join the conspiracy.

Great art and popularity, in the theatre as elsewhere, have nothing whatever to do with each other. Great art may be popular or it may not be, but in either case its popularity is no reflection of its greatness. A great play cannot survive in the theatre unless it has a quality which, as we have seen, it shares with every indifferent play that succeeds. But given this, it may for a variety of reasons still fail. Theatrically, it may hold and even please The Audience, but it may be too sad or too provocative, too daring or too quiet, even too long or too short, to attract the very large public necessary to keep a theatre open for a long time. Stageworthy plays that are fine fail as often as they succeed in competition with stageworthy plays that are not; but the dramatist who can write fine plays will never better his chances in the theatre by trimming. The public prints are full of warnings against what is called 'high-brow' drama, but the fact remains that when a dramatist of genius storms and captures the theatre he never does it by ceasing to be high-brow, if that distasteful word means intelligent beyond the anticipation of The Audience. Mr. Shaw and Mr. Galsworthy are high-brow dramatists, and they could never be anything else, though they should go on writing plays that ran a year apiece till doomsday. They and their like are glad of as much attention from The Audience as they can get, but they are not going to conform to the wishes of The Audience in order to get it. They are as greedy as anyone else of applause so long as it can be had on their own terms. There are their plays, and The Audience can take them or leave them, it being greatly to the credit of The Audience that as often as not it takes them. But when it comes to a question of treating The Audience not only as a dispenser of highly desirable rewards, but also as a dictator, you must apply elsewhere. We playgoers have a great deal in our hands, but we should be wary of being persuaded that we have everything. We can have the artist in the theatre, or we can keep him out; but we have to learn that it is as an artist, that is to say as an original mind beyond our legislation, that he will stay if he is to stay at all.

THE BORDER LINE

I HAVE, for the purpose of argument in this essay, drawn a somewhat definite line between two types of play. I am aware that in actual experience of the theatre it is often difficult to preserve the distinction as sharply as that. While I do not believe that the good dramatists ever compromise as to the integrity of their work, there unquestionably are dramatists who are able to achieve no more than a fitful sincerity. They lack that essential rigour of mind that characterises the big men and somehow informs even their least effective productions, but they have moods of insight and fugitive tidings of truth that will lift a moment or a scene from mediocrity to distinction on the stage, or sometimes give an undertone of vitality to a whole play. In such cases of confused accomplishment, our judgment is likely to remain confused also. There are plays, again, of apparently fine quality that miss their mark on account of faults that seem to be accidental and are yet probably significant of real defects in the dramatist's mind. We feel about the defects that we could put them right in half an hour, but on closer examination we should no doubt discover that they were involved in the texture of the work; though there are certainly plays that fail on the stage from lack of technical experience, which is a convincing argument in favour of experimental theatres that can afford to let young dramatists see their apprentice work in action. If I were myself a beginner at playwriting and had no theatre in which to find out what my mistakes chiefly were, I would worry my friends into giving me some sort of a performance in the back parlour. Yet again, there are plays of which, however trained our perceptions may be, we cannot be quite sure that we have seen an adequate production. A cast of famous players may do something so skilfully as to obscure the fact that they are doing entirely the wrong thing. This is not their fault, but that of the producer, and of the dramatist himself who ought to have too firm a control of his theatre to allow such miscarriages of dramatic justice. In any case I am sure that I have seen alleged performances of plays that were not what the dramatist intended at all. It may very well have been that his intention was impossible to realise on the stage, but as to that we have no means of deciding in the theatre. We can only suspect now and again in the presence of a failure that it might have been otherwise.

Much more subtle is the doubt that will sometimes overtake us as to whether a play is really sincere or not. Sincerity is one of the few things that is easier to define accurately than to recognise with complete certainty. I have, I hope, made it clear in this essay what I conceive sincerity to be, and in most cases it is unmistakable when it appears. But it is not always so. It may be argued that if it does not immediately assert itself, and in the theatre of all places, it is not there, but I confess that for myself this is not always a satisfactory test. The uncertainty is rare, but not unknown. I am, for example, not at all sure what I really think about two very celebrated plays, 'Diplomacy' and 'Romance.' Both plays are masterpieces of theatrical effectiveness, but are they more than that? To be that alone would entitle them to respect, for skill of this kind is sufficiently rare, and to speak of it slightingly is to be slight oneself. But are they beyond that truly made out of the discovery of their authors, or by the adroit manipulation of discoveries already made? I am inclined to think that in both cases there is a good deal more sincerity than is commonly recognised by the more expensive monthly magazines,[1] though the style of neither play — I can speak of 'Diplomacy' in translation only — is quite convincing in the matter. If as a critic I had to apply my mind steadily to the question I might come to some definite conclusion for which I could advance logical reasons, but the playgoer is not called upon to do this, and here are two plays from which as a playgoer I come

[1] In case anybody should not know it, the phrase is Wilde's.

away having enjoyed every minute — or nearly every minute — in the theatre, and yet with doubts as to what their true quality is. Think of them in conjunction with manifestly great plays, and there is something wrong with them; but think of them in conjunction with obvious rubbish, and there is at once much in them that is notably right. Which all amounts to saying that, however clear-cut our theories about drama may be, there are occasions when it is extremely difficult to apply them pat in the theatre.

CREDO

I SHOULD like to summarise the views here advanced, in a confession of faith. Thus, I believe:

1. That the foundation of the English (or the English-speaking) theatre is the drama of the spoken word, as developed by Shakespeare and his fellows from the mysteries, moralities, and miracle plays, inherited and modified by the Restoration, kept in continuous use by inferior writers for nearly two hundred years, and invested again with its proper dignity during the past thirty.

2. That, consequently, the position of the theatre as the home of a great art depends always upon its relation to the best writers of the time. If it attracts them, drama will flourish and be constantly renewed in imaginative life; if it neglects them, drama will become insignificant.

3. That the decision rests with the actors. If they are determined to dominate the theatre, they can do so. But if they truly understand the nature of their own beautiful craft they know that it can be fully realised only in the service of fine drama. That the actor will give a performance of greater intrinsic acting value in a good part than in a poor

one, no matter how important the poor one may be in its own play.

4. That the purpose of the actors, first, last and all the time, should be to give an exact representation of the dramatist's intention, without too much anxiety about interpretation. That a producer is necessary to coördinate their efforts to this end. That the dramatist's intention is best expressed by his own text and not by what someone else may consider to be an improvement on it.[1]

5. That the distinction between realism and imagination in the theatre is a false one. That no play is realistic in any sense that will bear investigation. That the real distinction is between mechanical and organic plays.

6. That the theatre as a place of popular entertainment appeals to our relaxed moods, and is in competition with the cinema, the music-halls, the prize-ring, the Football Association and the Rugby Union, and all other inducements to pleasant loafing. That as such it is worth its living so long as it

[1] Recently Our Own Correspondent from Oxford writing in a Sunday paper of a forthcoming production of *King Lear* by the O.U.D.S. concluded thus: 'M. Komisarjevsky has made extensive cuts in the text; speculation is rife as to their nature. In short, the production promises to be a big success, and people who have not already booked their seats may have to go begging.' I may say that I greatly admire M. Komisarjevsky as a producer; but it is somewhat late in the day to stake his claim to the authorship of *King Lear*.

can make it, but that no one but its backers cares much what happens to it, since if it collapses, which is unlikely, its place will be taken by something else.

7. That the theatre of the imagination is in competition with nothing. That it will never be supported day in and day out by the great public, but that there are enough people who care tenaciously for it to enable it to carry on so long as it continues to interest some of the best writers; and that if it disappeared nothing could take its place. That the fact of its having kept going for more than twenty-five years since its revival encourages the hope that it will last a long time yet before passing into another period of eclipse.

8. That the playgoer is both an individual and part of The Audience. That in the former capacity his opinion may be worth listening to. That in the latter, he holds the purse strings, but that this is no excuse for telling him that he is the fellow who knows best.

9. That in criticism good manners are consistent with honesty, and a sense of proportion with personal dignity.[1]

[1] Mr. Dukes, in the book above mentioned, says surprisingly as advancing the critic's position, 'A good criticism will live longer than a poor play.' Doubtless. So will a good donkey than a sick horse. But we should not fancy the chances of the noblest moke in the Derby. Not, I beg leave to state, that I would call any critic a donkey.

10. That the level of acting and stage production to-day is very high, and that in spite of occasional turns of bad luck the dramatists are mostly themselves to blame when their plays fail in the theatre.

11. That in the theatre, as elsewhere, theory does not govern art, but is deduced from the practice of the artists.

12. That, to close as we began, the end of our desire in the theatre is for a fine play loyally acted by a well-chosen and well-directed cast, and that beside this all other considerations are of no account.

THE END

INDEX OF NAMES